MW00989243

PETER F. DRUCKER'S

THE **Five**

MOST IMPORTANT

QUESTIONS

Self-Assessment Tool

IRD EDITION

ACILITATOR'S GUIDE

Leader
to Leader
INSTITUTE

JOSSEY-BASS
A Wiley Imprint
www.josseybass.com

Published by Jossey-Bass
A Wiley Imprint
989 Market Street, San Francisco, CA 94103-1741—www.josseybass.com

Readers should be aware that Internet Web sites offered as citations and/or sources for further information may have changed or disappeared between the time this was written and when it is read.

Limit of Liability/Disclaimer of Warranty: While the publisher and author have used their best efforts in preparing this book, they make no representations or warranties with respect to the accuracy or completeness of the contents of this book and specifically disclaim any implied warranties of merchantability or fitness for a particular purpose. No warranty may be created or extended by sales representatives or written sales materials. The advice and strategies contained herein may not be suitable for your situation. You should consult with a professional where appropriate. Neither the publisher nor author shall be liable for any loss of profit or any other commercial damages, including but not limited to special, incidental, consequential, or other damages.

Jossey-Bass books and products are available through most bookstores. To contact Jossey-Bass directly call our Customer Care Department within the U.S. at 800-956-7739, outside the U.S. at 317-572-3986, or fax 317-572-4002.

Jossey-Bass also publishes its books in a variety of electronic formats. Some content that appears in print may not be available in electronic books.

Facilitator's Guide ISBN: 978-0-470-53123-5
Participant Workbook ISBN: 978-0-470-53121-1

Printed in the United States of America
THIRD EDITION
PB Printing 10 9 8 7 6 5 4 3 2 1

Contents

About This Package

The Five Most Important Questions Self-Assessment Tool package consists of three components:

- This *Facilitator's Guide*

- The *Participant Workbook*

- The book *The Five Most Important Questions You Will Ever Ask About Your Organization*

Each of these is described here in more detail.

The Facilitator's Guide

The *Facilitator's Guide* is intended for organizational leaders, as well as facilitators and consultants, who would like to learn how to improve or achieve performance excellence using Peter F. Drucker's Five Most Important Questions or *Self-Assessment Tool*.

The *Guide* explains how to engage organizations in self-assessment, from introducing The Five Most Important Questions to the organization to deepening practical experience with self-assessment. The *Guide* details steps for organizational leaders (board chairs, chief executive officers, and executives), consultants, and professional facilitators to design self-assessment for the organization, as well as conduct an introductory workshop on self-assessment.

The *Guide* offers both structure and flexibility; shows how to be inclusive yet efficient; and reflects principles of good governance, sound management, and effective group process.

The *Guide* contains the following sections.

Section 1: Organizational Self-Assessment

Section 1 provides resources and the steps necessary to design and conduct a basic organizational self-assessment. The following are the major steps:

Gain commitment: Introduce self-assessment to the board for commitment and approval

Design self-assessment: Form a Self-Assessment Team and design a detailed process

Conduct self-assessment: Gather and analyze data; prepare for and engage in facilitated dialogue

Take action: Approve, implement, and appraise the strategic and operational plans

   This section shows you how to design facilitated dialogue sessions as well as how to use data collection and analysis to inform your self-assessment.

Section 2: Introductory Workshop Preparation

We have designed full-day and half-day introductory workshops that can be delivered by organizational leaders or professional facilitators. The workshop provides a foundation for organizations to conduct self-assessment either on their own or with a facilitator. This section provides background information on The Five Most Important Questions model in workshop scenarios, as well as resources to help you design and prepare a workshop.

   We also provide a two-day workshop option that covers the introductory material as well but allows more time for participants to familiarize themselves with the self-assessment process.

Section 3: Introductory Workshop Script

This section takes you step-by-step through the workshop and prepares you to deliver the information participants will need to conduct self-assessment. Also available (at www.josseybass.com/go/druckersat) is an accompanying Microsoft PowerPoint™ presentation for you to use as you conduct the workshop.

The Participant Workbook

The Five Most Important Questions Participant Workbook is used to guide individual thinking and prepare participants for meaningful and productive discussion and decision making.[1] It describes each of The Five Most Important Questions and contains worksheets to help organizations use Drucker's framework to revisit the mission, set direction, and take action. The *Workbook* can be used as preparation for the introductory workshop or organizational self-assessment or as a stand-alone workbook for individuals for leadership development or self-reflection.

The Book

The book *The Five Most Important Questions You Will Ever Ask About Your Organization* presents an overview of Peter Drucker's The Five Most Important Questions with insight on the questions and on Drucker from six prominent thought leaders—Jim Collins, Philip Kotler, James Kouzes, Judith Rodin, V. Kasturi Rangan, and Frances Hesselbein. The book should be read by any organizational leader or facilitator who will be conducting the self-assessment process. This book is recommended *pre-reading* for the introductory workshop or for participants or decision makers considering one.

About the Self-Assessment Process

Initially developed for small to mid-sized nonprofit organizations, the *Self-Assessment Tool* has been used successfully by nonprofit organizations of all sizes and types, as well as by corporations and government agencies that collaborate or partner with the social sector.

The *Self-Assessment Tool*

- Is easy to use and easy to complete within a short period of time

- Clearly explains and demonstrates Peter F. Drucker's management principles and their application to social sector organizations, their partners, or any organization with a socially responsible mission and multiple bottom lines

- Forces clarity of thinking by asking participants to observe trends, listen to the customer, and focus on results

- Emphasizes a commitment to action, as well as ongoing performance appraisal

- Supplements the organization's existing strategic planning and evaluation processes

The moment one seriously considers The Five Most Important Questions, the experience of the Drucker "method" begins. It is much more than answering questions. The Drucker self-assessment process converts knowledge into effective action.

Who's Involved

Self-assessment brings leaders in an organization together to explore questions that focus long-term strategy and strategic planning. The process engages leadership on all levels in a challenging process of organizational self-discovery. The board chairman and chief executive lead the effort.

As everyone who has been involved in a process of self-assessment or planning knows, the quality of that process becomes every bit as important as the discoveries themselves. The success and impact of self-assessment rely on *effective* and *informed* dialogue.

To ensure that dialogue is *effective*, a facilitator, trainer, or consultant, well-versed in The Five Most Important Questions, provides essential guidance to any self-assessment implementation by seeing that different points of view are expressed during the process.

To ensure that dialogue is *informed*, organizations involve in the process leaders dispersed throughout the organization, including the board and management team, as well as staff, volunteers, and customers.

Ease of Use

The *Self-Assessment Tool* is easy to learn and use. The process does not require a significant amount of training to implement. The instructional *Participant Workbook* helps leaders in organizations explore The Five Most Important Questions both individually and in group discussions.

The *Tool*'s flexibility in process design brings minimal disruption to planning and operations, in comparison with other strategy and strategic planning tools. Simple designs can be used to refocus the mission, assess new opportunities, and set direction in a short amount of time (three to six months). Meanwhile, more complex designs that require longer periods of time can be developed.

The process is flexible. This *Guide* focuses on organizational self-assessment, but the process can be conducted in many different ways. For instance, the facilitated dialogue can take the form of an offsite strategy or strategic planning retreat, or it can be built into daily work, program, and project activities to improve performance. The *Tool* even can be used by individuals for leadership development and self-reflection.

Organizational leaders and facilitators are invited to download and use the color PowerPoint presentation shown in this guide. Other online materials available in customizable MS Word format include sample purpose and goals statements and sample full-day, half-day, and two-day training agendas.

Find additional resources, helpful tools, and information on The Five Most Important Questions at **www .leadertoleader.org/tools**

Foreword

An Adventure of Organizational Self-Discovery

Self-assessment is a process of organizational self-discovery. It is a discussion about the future and how your organization will shape it, an intellectual and emotional adventure—for minds and hearts are involved. The *Drucker Self-Assessment Tool* is designed to guide and focus this journey into the future with Peter Drucker's Five Most Important Questions: What is our mission? Who is our customer? What does the customer value? What are our results? and What is our plan? To answer these questions, you will look outside the organization to opportunities and to what your customers value. And you will look inside to the organization's mission and to what you must do to achieve results.

The *Self-Assessment Tool* is flexible. As one customer describes it, "This is a living, breathing process of examination, improvement, and reexamination." The *Tool* is used by organizations in the public, private, and social sectors, and portions of it are woven into a range of planning exercises. Here are four examples that demonstrate the *Tool*'s use:

- A task force within a national public health organization had been wrestling for months over the proper focus and design of a proposed network of research centers. The chairman reports, "Once we stepped back and affirmed the research centers' mission, defined our primary and supporting customers, and identified what they value, we had a new understanding and were quickly able to come to a decision all could support."

- Newly elected members join a suburban county's library board every two years. The board's semi-annual orientation and planning retreat begins with Peter Drucker's questions and worksheets on mission. Said one member, "I have served on many boards, and I find it very healthy that in my first meeting there was sufficient time spent on the core reason this institution exists."

- A small community development agency used the *Tool* to conduct an organizational self-assessment in the face of rapidly changing community demographics. The executive director reflects on the resulting plan, "It was a lot of work, but it was satisfying work. The beauty of this structure is that it doesn't stop at the 'preferred future.' The methodology made the plan real and not just another brainstorming exercise."

- The *Tool* provided the format for field projects in an MBA course titled "Organizational Management and Leadership." The students' "clients" included nonprofit organizations, businesses, a government agency, and two universities. A student writes, "This has been the most important motivating factor in helping me determine what I want to pursue once I graduate." The professor comments, "The projects helped organizations develop action plans that would make them more effective in the community or the business world."

Whatever your purpose for using the *Tool,* you can adapt the self-assessment process to the needs and culture of your organization. Make it your own.

A Journey into the Future

Remarkable opportunities exist for those who would lead their organizations and this country into a new kind of community—a community of healthy children, strong families, good education, decent housing, safe neighborhoods, and work that dignifies—all embraced by the diverse, cohesive community that cares about all of its people. These leaders will dare to see life and community whole. Rather than fret about a "shrinking piece of the old pie," organizations with vision and new mind-sets will forge relationships crossing the private, public, and social sectors to build partnerships and community. They will change lives.

Peter Drucker's Five Most Important Questions go to the very heart of an organization—why it exists and how it will make a difference. They are the essential questions, and by asking them you will focus on excellence in performance and on what you must do to achieve it. The questions are not easy. We members of the Leader to Leader Institute board and staff ask them of ourselves periodically, and I know that when you ask these questions, all who participate in seeking answers will have an exuberant and valuable discussion.

The self-assessment process is an adventure in organizational self-discovery, a means for assessing how to be: how to develop quality, character, mind-set, values, and courage. On behalf of the Leader to Leader Institute, we offer this guide to your journey into the future and our encouragement to begin.

September 2010

Frances Hesselbein
President and Chief Executive Officer
Leader to Leader Institute
(founded as the Peter F. Drucker
Foundation for Nonprofit Management)

Introduction
by Peter F. Drucker[2]

Editor's Note: Though this introduction was written over ten years ago, Drucker's points and his concepts are amazingly as relevant as ever—if not more today—to our society, social sector organizations, and to any organization with a socially driven mission.

Social sector institutions are America's resounding success story of the last fifty years. They are central to the quality of life, central to citizenship, and indeed carry the values of American society and the American tradition. The pressure for effective community service will only grow as society continues through a period of sharp transformation. Out of a need for personal involvement, the number of Americans who volunteer will increase as well. The social sector organization is fast becoming the new center of social action, of active commitment, and of meaningful contribution.

An accomplished fact in today's environment, and a very healthy one, is the requirement that social sector organizations be accountable. *Changed lives* is the non-profit organization's "bottom line." Each mission must be thought through in terms of results, and the organization must document the difference that is being made in society and in the lives of individuals. People are no longer simply interested to know, Is it a good cause? Instead, they want to see both commitment *and* competence—a demonstration of achievement as a responsible and effective organization.

The Five Most Important Questions

The self-assessment process is a method for assessing what you are doing, why you are doing it, and what you *must* do to improve an organization's performance. It asks the five essential questions, *What is our mission? Who is our customer? What does the customer value? What are our results?* and *What is our plan?* Self-assessment leads to action and lacks meaning without it. To meet growing needs and succeed in a turbulent and exacting environment, social sector organizations must focus on mission, demonstrate accountability, and achieve results.

You cannot arrive at the right definition of results without significant input from your *customers*—and please do not get into a debate over that term. In business, a customer is someone you must satisfy. If you don't, you have no results. And pretty soon you have no business. In a nonprofit organization, whether you call the customer a student, patient, member, participant, volunteer, donor, or anything else, the focus must be on what these individuals and groups value—on satisfying their needs, wants, and aspirations.

The danger is in acting on what *you* believe satisfies the customer. You will inevitably make wrong assumptions. Leadership should not even try to guess at the answers; it should always go to customers in a systematic quest for those answers. And so, in the self-assessment process, you will have a three-way conversation with your board, staff, and customers and include each of these perspectives in your discussions and decisions.

Planning Is Not an Event

When you follow the self-assessment process through to its completion, you will have formulated a plan. Planning is frequently misunderstood as making future decisions, but decisions exist only in the present. You must have overarching goals that add up to a vision for the future, but the immediate question that faces the organization is not what to do tomorrow. The question is, What must we do *today* to achieve results? Planning is not an event. It is the continuous process of strengthening what works and abandoning what does not, of making risk-taking decisions with the greatest knowledge of their potential effect, and of setting objectives, appraising performance and results through systematic feedback, and making ongoing adjustments as conditions change.

The First Action Requirement of Leadership

Your organization's commitment to self-assessment is a commitment to leadership development. You have vital judgments ahead: whether to change the mission, what opportunities match your competence and commitment, how you will build community and change lives. Self-assessment—this constant resharpening, constant refocusing—is the first action requirement of leadership.

In my fifty years of work with social sector organizations, I have known many outstanding leaders. One is a man I met quite by chance, a rabbi, who taught me by example that *"you are responsible for allocating your life."* This is as true for organizations as it is for individuals. It is the underlying challenge of the self-assessment process. The questions must continually be asked, Why does the organization exist? What, in the end, do we want to be remembered for? When you find answers, above all, I urge you to act on them.

August 1998   Peter F. Drucker
                                                                   Claremont, California

Section 1
Organizational Self-Assessment

The *Self-Assessment Tool* is flexible and can be adapted to meet a variety of planning and leadership needs. This guide focuses on organizational self-assessment, strategic planning for the total organization, but you also can apply the *Tool* to programs and projects, or to test innovation.

Use this section to determine the level of preparation and resources your organization requires to conduct self-assessment. If you are not familiar with the *Tool*, it will be helpful to familiarize yourself with the *Participant Workbook* before you begin designing self-assessment for your organization.

Communicating Self-Assessment to the Organization

Organizational self-assessment leads to performance excellence. You will develop and implement a plan that may change the way your organization thinks and operates. Before starting self-assessment and throughout the process, it is important to communicate the process to your organization regularly through meetings, announcements, and updates. Points may include

- Your organization's purpose for undertaking self-assessment

- An overview of self-assessment and the process you have developed

- Introductions, as appropriate, of facilitators and members of the Self-Assessment Team

- Progress reports

- Final outcomes (mission, goals, and the plan of work)

Engage in a dialogue with the people in your organization to gain an understanding of how self-assessment impacts daily efforts, as well as how the process can be improved.

Governance and Management in Self-Assessment[3]

Organizational self-assessment is built on a bedrock principle for nonprofit organizations and many others: the clear and sharp differentiation of governance and management. The board of directors, trustees, or governors is responsible for the governance and policy of the organization. Management is accountable for the objectives and performance.

Operating within these broad guidelines allows social sector organizations to achieve their highest performance. With the chairman of the board and the chief executive officer setting the standard for a productive partnership, the organization can focus on changing lives and building community.

Table 1 shows a broad outline of the responsibilities of the board and the accountabilities of management during self-assessment.

TABLE 1. ORGANIZATIONAL SELF-ASSESSMENT.

Responsibilities of the Board	Accountabilities of Management
Leadership The chairman recommends self-assessment to the board, leads the effort, and presents the outcomes of self-assessment (mission, goals, and plan) to the board for approval.	*Leadership* The CEO coordinates self-assessment and ensures that the organization reaches desired outcomes as directed by the board.
Strategic Planning The board uses self-assessment to determine direction and the allocation of resources.	*Operational (Tactical) Planning* Management uses self-assessment to develop the operational plan, which details the objectives, action steps, and budget the organization will use to achieve goals and further the mission.
Appraisal and Oversight The board uses the principles of self-assessment to appraise performance. It reviews annual and interim management reports. As the legal steward of the organization the board carries the fiduciary responsibility and ensures compliance with laws and standards of practice.	*Performance* Management uses the principles of self-assessment to implement the plan and achieve results. Accountable for performance, it reports to the board on progress and presents annual and interim management reports.

Figure 1 uses a circular design to show that planning—and appraisal—is continuous.

FIGURE 1. PLANNING FOR RESULTS DIAGRAM.

The Planning Process[4]

Mission is essential to social sector planning. The mission answers the questions, "What is our reason for being?" "Why do we do what we do?" "What, in the end, do we want to be remembered for?" From the mission flow goals that set the organization's fundamental long-range direction and, together, outline its desired future. Objectives are specific and measurable levels of achievement. Action steps are the detailed plans and activities to meet the objectives, the budget commits necessary resources, and appraisal demonstrates whether objectives are met and results achieved.

Process Guidelines

Organizational self-assessment can take from three to six months to conduct. The process requires board approval and commitment, so it is wise to coordinate self-assessment with your board's meeting and planning schedule. The following steps will help you design self-assessment (Figure 2).

FIGURE 2. ORGANIZATIONAL SELF-ASSESSMENT.

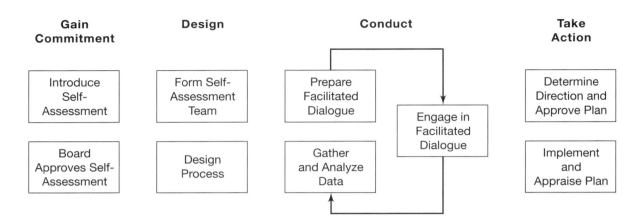

Gain commitment: Introduce self-assessment to the board for commitment and approval.

Design: Form a Self-Assessment Team and design a detailed process.

Conduct: Gather and analyze data. Prepare for and engage in facilitated dialogue.

Take action: Approve, implement, and appraise the strategic and operational plans.

Gain Commitment

Board commitment to self-assessment fulfills a fundamental responsibility of governance. As trustees of the organization, the board is responsible for the vision, the mission, and the strategic goals of the organization, as well as oversight of performance and allocation of resources.

Organizational self-assessment requires the participation of the board and the management team. The formal decision to initiate the process is made by the board of directors. It is the responsibility of the chairman to propose self-assessment to the board. Once the process is approved, the chairman of the board and the chief executive officer (CEO) lead the effort. It is the responsibility of the CEO to ensure that the process is effectively carried out.

The *Self-Assessment Tool* is designed to engage board members and management in strategic decision making. Board meetings at which self-assessment is proposed should allow sufficient time to address and discuss the following:

- *Purpose and expected results* for undertaking self-assessment

- *Key elements to the process design:* estimated time, resources, and budget, as well as major steps

- *Roles and responsibilities* of the Self-Assessment Team

- *Elements essential to success,* such as

  - Utilizing an experienced facilitator to guide dialogue
  - Engaging dispersed leadership
  - Encouraging constructive dissent
  - Using data to inform dialogue

To introduce the organization to self-assessment the chairman of the board and the CEO can ask those approving and participating in the process to read Peter Drucker's *The Five Most Important Questions You Will Ever Ask About Your Organization.*

In addition, the organization can conduct a *self-assessment introductory workshop* (see Section 3). The workshop will familiarize your organization with the elements of the *Self-Assessment Tool,* the resources required to conduct self-assessment, and, most important, the power of self-assessment—how it strengthens strategic planning and organizational performance. A facilitator can deliver the workshop or a board or staff member can use the resources in Section 3 to deliver it.

Design

Your process design details the steps your organization will take to conduct self-assessment, starting with introducing self-assessment to the board and ending with implementing and appraising the plan. The design outlines who is responsible for completing assigned tasks and by when.

As you design your process, think through your organization's purpose for undertaking self-assessment, as well as what your board and management team expect to gain from the process. Use the major steps for self-assessment outlined in Figure 2 to estimate the resources, amount of time, and budget your organization will need to carry out the process.

Self-Assessment Team

The Self-Assessment Team includes those leading and managing self-assessment, as well as those participating in dialogue and organizational planning. The chairman of

TABLE 2. SELF-ASSESSMENT TEAM ROLES AND RESPONSIBILITIES.

Leadership	
Chairman of the board	Oversees self-assessment
	Introduces self-assessment to the board for approval
	Presents outcomes of self-assessment (vision, mission, goals, and plan) to the board for action
	Participates in facilitated dialogue
Chief executive officer (CEO)	Ensures self-assessment is carried out effectively
	Provides input to the strategic plan (vision, mission, and goals)
	Develops the operational plan (objectives, action steps, and budget)
	Participates in facilitated dialogue
Board	Approves self-assessment
	Uses self-assessment to revisit the mission, set the goals, and approve the plan
	Members may help in the design of self-assessment
	Members participate in facilitated dialogue
Facilitator	Facilitates and summarizes the dialogue
	May help
	Introduce self-assessment to the board
	Design the self-assessment process
	Gather and analyze data
Staff	May help
	Introduce self-assessment to the board
	Design and manage the self-assessment process
	Prepare the Self-Assessment Team for dialogue
	Gather and analyze data
	May participate in dialogue
Customer	Provides customer information
	May participate in facilitated dialogue

the board and the chief executive officer form the Self-Assessment Team and determine roles. Table 2 outlines common roles and responsibilities. Use it to guide how you build your Self-Assessment Team.

Facilitated Dialogue

At the heart of self-assessment is facilitated dialogue. Using the *Participant Workbook* to design and guide dialogue sessions, you will invite leaders in your organization to engage in intensive decision-making and direction-setting meetings. Major findings and recommendations generated during dialogue are used by your board and management team to revisit the mission, set goals, and develop the plan. The quality of your self-assessment depends on who you select to facilitate and participate in dialogue, as well as how you design your sessions.

Choosing a Facilitator

The facilitator plays a significant role in self-assessment. She or he guides your organization in exploring The Five Most Important Questions. The facilitator often helps introduce self-assessment to the organization and offers invaluable input to the design of self-assessment as a whole, as well as dialogue sessions.

Self-assessment calls for broad contribution from leaders dispersed throughout the organization. During dialogue, the facilitator ensures full participation, draws out different points of view, and encourages leaders to use constructive dissent to work through conflict. She or he keeps the Self-Assessment Team focused on developing the knowledge and information the organization needs to determine direction and take action. A good facilitator is

- *Results focused*—understands clearly what is to be accomplished during dialogue sessions, and communicates it to the group

- *A good listener*—listens closely to all discussions, asks related questions, probes for clarity, challenges inconsistent statements and reminds the Self-Assessment Team to use valid data to support ideas and decisions

- *Capable of exercising control while encouraging participation*—keeps the discussion moving among all participants and knows when and how to discourage those who monopolize the discussion, while encouraging others to share their points of view

- *An analytic and strategic thinker*—communicates the results of the discussion orally and in writing

- *Impartial and trustworthy*[5]

The organization may choose a facilitator who is either internal or external to the organization.

Internal. Using an inside facilitator—whether a board member, staff member, or volunteer—saves the time and complexity of orienting an outsider to the organization, and it makes good use of the organization's existing resources. Select a facilitator who will be objective and neutral throughout the process. The facilitator should understand Drucker's framework and language and be familiar with the *Tool.* The chairman of the board and the CEO *should not* facilitate. These key individuals need to participate fully in dialogue sessions.

External. Engaging a qualified outside facilitator or consultant brings proven expertise to the role and frees everyone within the organization to focus on other aspects of the process. An outside facilitator can be objective and neutral, which may make it easier for participants to be open. It is important for an outside facilitator to understand an organization's history, culture, and current performance before dialogue sessions start. Select a facilitator who has experience with The Five Most Important Questions and strategic planning.

Multiple. If your process design calls for a large number of group sessions, participants, or both—particularly if the organization is geographically dispersed—multiple facilitators may be used. One option may be for the organization to choose an outside facilitator to train and work with multiple inside facilitators. Make sure facilitators guide a consistent group of participants—to ensure continuity between dialogue sessions. Both internal and external facilitators must know and use Drucker's framework and language.[6]

Selecting Participants for Facilitated Dialogue

To generate productive dialogue, invite participants who bring a diversity of experience and knowledge to the conversation—strategic thinkers as well as those familiar with operations. Both are important to create balance between generating and exploring ideas and translating ideas into action.

For organizational self-assessment, it is essential the chairman of the board and the chief executive officer participate in the dialogue. It is recommended that the full board participates. For instances when board members cannot be present at a session, make sure you keep them informed and updated on the progress of self-assessment.

At any point you may ask leaders in your organization with specific knowledge and experience (program, policy, or fundraising) to participate. As you approach Question 5—"What is our plan?"—it is important to gather input from those who will be implementing the plan to help develop objectives, action steps, and budget. This builds commitment to mission and ownership of the plan.

Finally, self-assessment requires you to listen to your customers. You may ask volunteers, donors, or your primary customer to offer input for the sessions. Your customers might comprise people with different needs, preferences, and aspirations. All enrich the dialogue.

Designing Dialogue Sessions

Design the dialogue to explore each of The Five Most Important Questions in sequence. At any point, your team may revisit a question it already has explored. In particular, it is important to refer back to Question 1—"What is our mission?"— as you progress through each succeeding question. As you work with Question 5—"What is our plan?"—your board will determine and approve the strategic direction (mission and goals) before your organization develops and approves the operational plan (objectives, action steps, and budget).

Usually the dialogue is designed in a *series of sessions* that can span several weeks or months. Each session explores one of The Five Most Important Questions, although, at times, sessions may combine more than one question. Make sure you plan enough time before each session to gather and analyze data that will be useful to the facilitator and participants.

You may consider holding a *retreat* (offsite or onsite) to offer participants a more concentrated time to explore The Five Most Important Questions. A retreat allows participants to focus on self-assessment without distraction. It also may be more convenient for participants who have difficulty participating in a series of discussions due to scheduling and travel costs. The retreat format may be an excellent option for engaging your full board in self-assessment.

You may hold more than one retreat—for instance, two full-day retreats with time in between reserved for data analysis. The retreat format can be used as an alternative to holding multiple, shorter sessions, or it can be a part of a series of sessions.

Each dialogue session should have well-defined objectives that are aligned with your organization's purpose for conducting self-assessment. Use these objectives to create an agenda for each session and select worksheets from the *Participant Workbook* that will aid the discussion (see the sample agenda in the Appendix).

Data gathering and analysis will shape how you design dialogue sessions. Review the *Participant Workbook* to understand what type of data is needed for each question. For instance, Question 1—"What is our mission?"—and Question 3—"What does the customer value?"—call for an environmental scan and customer research, respectively. Think about how and when to present data to participants as they engage in self-assessment and plan accordingly.

Before your dialogue begins, allow sufficient time for your facilitator and participants to prepare. It is helpful for everyone to read through the *Participant Workbook*. Your facilitator may ask participants to complete selected worksheets from the *Participant Workbook* before engaging in dialogue. In addition, the Self-Assessment Team may conduct *depth interviews* with individuals who may or may not be participating in the dialogue. Depth interviews are one-on-one interviews used to highlight the insights of a select group of individuals within the organization. Interview findings provide a touchstone for facilitated discussion and decision making.

Recording and Summarizing the Dialogue

Dialogue summaries are used by the board and management team for planning sessions. Before your dialogue begins, think through how you would like to summarize your sessions. You may record sessions using notes as well as audio recordings. Work with your board and management team to develop a way to summarize notes and recordings so the information is easy to use during planning sessions. Typically, your facilitator records, drafts, and presents dialogue summaries to the Self-Assessment Team. A sample summary of a facilitated dialogue can be found in the Appendix.

Conduct

Once you have designed your process, you conduct self-assessment, which includes gathering and analyzing data that will inform discussion sessions and engage leaders in dialogue.

Data Gathering and Analysis

Dialogue in self-assessment is grounded in data analysis. It is important for you to plan in advance of dialogue sessions what information participants will require and how long it will take to develop, analyze, and summarize information. During the design step, the Self-Assessment Team assesses the quality of data your organization uses. It then identifies additional data-gathering and research requirements and assigns roles and responsibilities.

At times, the need to analyze data emerges from dialogue. For instance, while participants explore Question 3—"What does the customer value?"—they may discover the need to gather more information from the customer before moving to Question 4—"What are our results?" Reserve appropriate time between dialogue sessions if your organization needs to collect additional data.

Types of Data Used for Self-Assessment

Data used for self-assessment generally include internal data, depth interviews, the environmental scan, and customer research. Internal data and depth interviews provide background and context for discussion, while the environmental scan and customer research keep the dialogue focused on external trends, the customer, and results.

Internal Data. Internal data are summarized information regarding the history, present status, and performance of the organization. Internal data are gathered to orient the Self-Assessment Team as it designs and conducts self-assessment.[7] Data may include

- Current mission statement

- Information about the organization and its history

- Organizational structure

- Planning documents—the strategic and operational plans

- Performance-related reports—annual report, and so on

- Research and program evaluation

Depth Interviews. Depth interviews are one-on-one interviews used to highlight the insights of a select group of individuals within the organization. Interview findings provide a touchstone for facilitated discussion and decision making.[8] Worksheets and questions from the *Participant Workbook* may be used to conduct depth interviews with individuals who may or may not participate in dialogue. Usually the facilitator conducts and summarizes depth interviews. Depth interviews usually are conducted with individuals who

- Have views considered to be valuable for self-assessment

- May choose to hold back in group discussions

- Are known to increase their participation in a group setting if given advance opportunity to prepare

  To design depth interviews, the Self-Assessment Team

- Selects depth interview participants

- Designs questions

- Determines how the interviews will be conducted

- Summarizes results for facilitated dialogue[9]

A sample depth interview is provided in the Appendix.

Environmental Scan. The environmental scan allows you to discover the emerging trends that will have the greatest impact on the organization. It is used "to find and identify change . . . by examining the sources and direction of change as they become evident through [research], media, publications, and individual observation and experience."[10] Emerging trends may include

- Demographics of current and potential customers

- Community issues and conditions

- Cultural or social norms

- Economic and funding activity

- Policy, legislation, and regulation

- Technologies, models, and methods

Depending on its scale and complexity, the environmental scan may be designed and completed in a relatively short period of time or it may be a longer project. To design an environmental scan, the Self-Assessment Team

- Determines, as specifically as possible, what data it will analyze

- Identifies data sources *within* and *outside* the organization

- Develops methods for gathering and analyzing information

- Creates a plan to conduct and summarize the scan and assigns tasks[11]

Customer Research. The purpose of customer research is to bring the voice of the customer directly into the self-assessment process—"Who is our customer?" and "What does the customer value?" The scale and complexity of customer research depend on the needs and capacity of your organization. To design customer research, the Self-Assessment Team

- Determines what information it needs to gain from customers

- Identifies customer groups to engage (both current and potential)

- Designs research questions

- Determines how to conduct the study (surveys, focus groups, individual interviews, or statistical analysis)

- Decides who will lead the research

- Sets a timeline and budget and assigns tasks

The Self-Assessment Team may use researchers internal or external to the organization. The benefits of engaging external researchers are expertise and objectivity. The benefits of using internal researchers are familiarity and commitment to the organization, as well as cost-effectiveness. It is important for the organization to hear directly from customers what they value.

The Self-Assessment Team, and those responsible for data gathering and analysis, collaborate to draft a summary of findings. Reports typically state both general and detailed findings, which might include quantitative analyses, qualitative analyses, or both. Reports also cite sources and describe methods.[12]

Several sample customer research designs are provided in the Appendix.

Guidelines for Facilitated Dialogue

The discussion group process is characterized by *interaction.* All participants are encouraged to share their ideas and to respond, question, and agree or disagree with each other. The facilitator pays attention to group process—how the members of the group engage in discussion and make decisions. During dialogue, it is important to check the following elements of group process:[13]

- *Is communication among group members direct and open?* The facilitator encourages group members to take risks by helping them agree on a "safety zone" for the session, stressing that anything less than direct and honest participation will lead to less-optimal results.

- *Is there equal participation by group members, or do some dominate while others sit and listen?* The facilitator asks quiet members for their opinions or forms subgroups for discussions to encourage participation.

- *Does the group reach a consensus (all members agree on a decision and can agree to support it)?* Encouraging the members to work until they reach a consensus results in decisions or action plans that all members will support. The process of reaching a consensus helps the group establish clarity and commitment.

- *Do the group members focus on the topic at hand or become sidetracked (on details that allow them to avoid larger issues, on past mistakes rather than future solutions, and so forth)?* The facilitator keeps the group focused and encourages constructive dissent.

- *Does the group value the individual differences of the members and the roles that each person can play in the group?* The facilitator helps group members take on roles that improve the group's overall effectiveness.[14]

Recording Ideas During Sessions

Recording ideas and suggested action steps is an important job of the facilitator. This can be done with a flip chart and whiteboard. Ideas should be displayed where all can see them. If the participant group is divided into smaller groups for discussions, ask the group members to take notes on their discussions so that they can report them back to the full group. Participants also may take notes in the *Participant Workbook*. A flip chart or whiteboard also is useful for creating lists of priorities, ratings, or rankings of items.

Take Action

Adopting the Plan

Your board and management team use what is learned during facilitated dialogue to develop the strategic and operational plans. First, the board revisits the mission and determines the goals. The chairman of the board presents a finalized strategic plan to the board for action. Adoption of a vision statement may be requested as part of the strategic plan, if one has been developed.

Once the mission and goals have been approved, the chief executive officer, with input from the staff, develops the objectives, action steps, and budget that will be used to further the mission and achieve the goals. Following a board presentation and discussion, the chairman will request that the board approve the operational plan. As soon as approval is given, implementation begins.

Implementing the Plan

For self-assessment to be effective, your organization *must* commit itself to take action and implement the plan. You should gain this commitment before engaging in self-assessment. As you implement the plan, your organization will continue to use the principles of The Five Most Important Questions to prepare your organization to take action.

The first step is to communicate the plan. The chairman of the board and chief executive officer demonstrate their commitment to performance excellence through sharing what is new to prepare the organization for strategic and operational change. The board and the management team deepen this commitment when they also communicate the plan to volunteers, staff, donors, and the customers.

Communication will take various forms, such as holding meetings and sending informational and status reports. Ensure that communication is interactive so that the plan is clear and questions can be answered.

Alongside communication, the organization's leadership must prepare people for new roles, assignments, and processes. Make clear assignments and establish systems to monitor and review performance. Staff performance must be tied directly to organizational performance.

Finally, the organization should remain consistent in appraising the plan. If the plan needs to be adjusted, the chief executive officer and the management team will reallocate resources to strengthen what is working well, improve what is weak, and abandon what is not producing results. Use Drucker's principles to encourage your staff to appraise performance and identify course corrections. In this way, all levels of your organization will recognize opportunities to improve performance and your organization will become more effective in its commitment to serve the customer.

Section 2
Introductory Workshop Preparation

We have designed a workshop to introduce self-assessment to board chairmen and chief executive officers of social sector organizations and their partners. The workshop provides organizations a foundation for conducting self-assessment, either on their own or with the support of a professional facilitator.

To effectively introduce self-assessment, it is essential for you to understand the underlying principles and language of Peter Drucker's self-assessment process. Reading Drucker's book *The Five Most Important Questions You Will Ever Ask About Your Organization* (Jossey-Bass, 2008) will help with this. You also should be familiar or familiarize yourself with how to use The Five Most Important Questions as a framework, so that you can help guide other leaders or your own organization to design basic organizational self-assessment and facilitate dialogue. Therefore, you should carefully read through all the components of this package prior to conducting the workshop.

Purpose and Goals

The overarching goal of this introductory workshop is to provide the leaders involved in the workshop a foundation for conducting self-assessment on their own.

Purpose

Learn how to conduct self-assessment to lead your organization toward *performance excellence*.

Goals

- Understand the underlying principles and terminology of The Five Most Important Questions

- Gain experience with the *Self-Assessment Tool*

- Bring the *Tool* to your organization

Copies of the purpose and goals are available on the Web at www.josseybass .com/go/druckersat so that you can customize them to fit the specific needs of your workshop. Find additional resources at www.leadertoleader.org/tools

Target Audiences and Design Options

For self-assessment to be successful, the board chairman and chief executive officer, president, or executive director of an organization *must* champion or lead self-assessment. (For more information on the role of governance and management in self-assessment, please refer to Section 1.)

The introductory workshop is designed for organizational leaders to learn the basics of organizational self-assessment. It also is appropriate for facilitators and consultants who focus on strategic planning to attend an introductory workshop. The workshop may be led by an organizational leader or a facilitator.

Following are several design options for the introductory workshop.

Option 1: Board Chairman and CEO–Led Workshop, Single Organization

Social sector leaders can introduce self-assessment to members of their own organizations. The board chairman and chief executive officer can initiate and design the introductory workshop. They can either lead the workshop themselves or assign the facilitator role internally to someone skilled in facilitation. If the latter is the case, the board chairman and the chief executive officer *should* participate in the workshop so they can deepen their knowledge of self-assessment and how it works.

The board chairman and chief executive officer invite participants to the workshop. Board members must be invited. Other participants may include the management team, staff, donors, partners, and customers.

The benefits of this option include the following:

- The organization develops in-house knowledge of self-assessment.

- The organization can adapt the workshop for its own specific needs and considerations.

- The introductory workshop can be part of a larger self-assessment design or process.

Option 2: Facilitator-Led Workshop, Single Organization

Similar to the first option, this option allows the facilitator to work with the members of one organization.

The benefits of this option include the following:

- An experienced professional facilitator can work with one organization with more depth and care, bringing in knowledge of how other organizations have approached, succeeded, or failed with self-assessment.

- A skilled facilitator asks hard questions and pushes for answers while serving as a neutral voice from outside of the organization.

- The workshop can be used to launch the organization into a longer-term self-assessment process.

Option 3: Facilitator-Led Workshop, Multiple Organizations

Facilitators can introduce The Five Most Important Questions to multiple organizations. The chairman and chief executive officer of each organization should be invited to attend, or they can ask a representative from their organization to attend. Other organizational members, as appropriate, can also attend.

The benefits of this option include the following:

- Facilitators can reach multiple organizations at once, and possibly, organizations involved in a partnership or collaboration.

- Participants can learn from the diversity and experience of the group.

- The versatility of the *Tool* is showcased as leaders explore how self-assessment can be uniquely applied to their organizations.

Although the language just used to describe the audience applies mostly to social sector organizations, other organizations with a mission that is socially beneficial can take advantage of this process as well.

Option 4: Facilitator-Led Workshop, Facilitators and Consultants

A facilitator may lead the workshop for other facilitators and consultants who focus on strategic planning on the organizational level. The facilitators can then help the organizations with which they work conduct self-assessment.

Pre-Work

Prior to the workshop, you should familiarize yourself with all of the package components and carefully review the script and slides and make notations of any changes for your audience.

Copies of the book *The Five Most Important Questions You Will Ever Ask About Your Organization* should be distributed to participants in advance, with instructions for them to read the book to familiarize themselves with The Five Most Important Questions and to bring it with them to the workshop.

As an option, you could also distribute the *Participant Workbook* in advance, giving participants an opportunity to review this material prior to the workshop as well. If you're trying to conserve time during the workshop, you can also assign selected worksheets as pre-work.

If the *Workbooks* are distributed in advance, be sure to instruct participants to bring their *Workbooks* with them to the workshop.

Agendas

We've provided sample agendas for full-day, half-day, and two-day versions of the introductory workshop. Copies of the agendas are available on the Web at www .josseybass.com/go/druckersat so that you can customize them to fit the specific needs of your workshop. Find additional resources at www.leadertoleader.org/tools

Full-Day Workshop

In the full-day workshop, you will present the framework of The Five Most Important Questions, along with the principles and language that support it. Some time will be spent on discussing how the tool was developed.

The workshop is designed for participants to familiarize themselves with and "experience" The Five Most Important Questions. You will have time to introduce key concepts for each question. Then you will engage participants in group activities during which they will use selected worksheets from the *Participant Workbook* to explore each question.

For each question, participants will have the opportunity to think about how to design self-assessment to meet the needs of their own organization. You will be recording some of these design steps on a whiteboard or flip chart.

Once you are finished with exploring the questions, you will ask participants to reflect on how Drucker's framework has changed participants' approaches to strategic thinking. This segues into the final workshop exercise, in which participants create a more detailed design for organizational self-assessment.

Half-Day Workshop

The half-day workshop presents the same content as the full-day workshop, but allows for less time to cover each section. As facilitator, you should try to move through the content presentation quickly, perhaps asking participants to hold their questions. You may also need to eliminate or shorten some of the exercises. The introductory workshop script in Section 3 includes notations regarding which exercises are most essential.

The goals of the half-day session are to present a content overview, explore the critical concept of dialogue, and give participants a chance to familiarize themselves with the *Participant Workbook* and worksheets, which should include a discussion of how participants can design self-assessment for their organizations. Although this will be a brief session, you want participants to leave feeling excited about the prospect of implementing this process in their organizations.

Because participants will not have as much time to explore all five questions during the session, you might recommend that they take additional time to explore the questions in more depth prior to designing and conducting organizational self-assessment.

Two-Day Workshop

The two-day workshop also presents the same content as the full-day workshop, but in an extended format. Additional time is allowed for discussion and exercises. If the two days are not scheduled consecutively, you could assign some homework to be completed in the intervening time. The first day will close with a discussion of the customer-related questions, so a good assignment would be for participants to collect some information about their customers and be prepared to share their learnings during the second session.

SAMPLE FULL-DAY AGENDA

Workshop Component	Estimated Time	Slides
Welcome, introductions, objectives	20 min.	1–11
Overview of self-assessment	45 min.	12–24
Break	15 min.	
What is our mission?	60 min.	25–36
Who is our customer?	45 min.	37–46
Lunch	60 min.	
What does the customer value?	45 min.	47–54
What are our results?	45 min.	55–64
What is our plan?	40 min.	65–74
Break	15 min.	
Reflect on The Five Most Important Questions	30 min.	75
Bring self-assessment to your organization	60 min.	76–78

SAMPLE HALF-DAY AGENDA

Workshop Component	Estimated Time	Slides
Welcome, introductions, objectives	20 min.	1–11
Overview of self-assessment	30 min.	12–24
What is our mission?	30 min.	25–36
Break	10 min.	
Who is our customer?	30 min.	37–46
What does the customer value?	20 min.	47–54
What are our results?	30 min.	55–64
What is our plan?	20 min.	65–74
Break	10 min.	
Reflect on The Five Most Important Questions	10 min.	75
Bring self-assessment to your organization	30 min.	76–78

SAMPLE TWO-DAY AGENDA

Workshop Component	Estimated Time	Slides
Day One		
Welcome, introductions, objectives	30 min.	1–11
Overview of self-assessment	45 min.	12–24
Break	15 min.	
What is our mission?	90 min.	25–36
Lunch	60 min.	
Who is our customer?	90 min.	37–46
What does the customer value?	90 min.	47–54
Break	15 min.	
Reflect on The Five Most Important Questions	40 min.	75

Workshop Component	Estimated Time	Slides
Day Two		
Review of Day One	15 min.	
What are our results?	90 min.	55–64
Break	15 min.	
What is our plan?	60 min.	65–74
Lunch	60 min.	
Reflect on The Five Most Important Questions	60 min.	75
Break	10 min.	
Bring self-assessment to your organization	90 min.	76–78

Supplies and Equipment Checklist

❑ A copy of the *Facilitator's Guide*

❑ A copy of the PowerPoint presentation (available at www.josseybass.com/go/druckersat)

❑ Computer, projector, and screen on which to display slides

❑ Flip chart or whiteboard and markers

❑ Masking tape if using a flip chart

❑ Extra paper or tablets and pens or pencils for each participant

❑ A copy of the agenda for each participant

❑ A copy of the purpose and objectives for each participant

❑ A copy of the *Participant Workbook* for each participant (may be distributed in advance of the workshop)

❑ A copy of the book *The Five Most Important Questions* for each participant (distributed in advance of the workshop)

Section 3

Introductory Workshop Script

There are three workshop options presented for the introductory self-assessment training: a half-day session, a full-day session, and a two-day session. Notes are provided in a full-day script that will help you adapt it for the half-day and two-day versions.

The sections of the script that focus on each of The Five Most Important Questions open with facilitator information—focus points and a list of related worksheets from the *Participant Workbook*. Note that an additional copy of each worksheet used for the workshops is provided in the *Participant Workbook*.

Before Participants Arrive

Facilitator Pre-Work

Read through the script and review additional resources for facilitators on the Web (at www.josseybass.com/go/druckersat and www.leadertoleader.org/tools), which includes a color PowerPoint slideshow that accompanies the script. Adapt the script and PowerPoint slides as needed. It is important for participants to spend as much time as possible experiencing self-assessment, so allocate as much time as you can to the group exercises in the script.

Once you know who is attending your workshop, create equal-sized groups of three to six participants. These groups will work through the Practical Application exercises, as well as the last two exercises, "Reflect on The Five Most Important Questions" and "Self-Assessment—Process Design."

Group work provides the opportunity for participants to experience first-hand what it is like to engage in facilitated dialogue, as well as how to design self-assessment for the organization. During the Practical Application exercises, participants will focus on *one* organization—see the following options.

Option 1: If a group comprises leaders from the same organization, arrange groups to reflect diversity, as well as dispersed leadership.

Option 2: If a group comprises leaders from different organizations, members should select one organization on which to focus. The leader of the organization that is selected should be comfortable with the group focusing on his or her organization. Make sure group composition reflects diversity and dispersed leadership (when possible).

Finally, prepare an evaluation to collect participant feedback at the end of your workshop.

Participant Pre-Work

Two weeks prior to the workshop, make sure participants receive a packet that includes

- A cover letter with the workshop logistics, purpose, and goals.

- One-page biographies as appropriate (workshop sponsors, facilitator, participants, and so on).

- The pre-read: *The Five Most Important Questions You Will Ever Ask About Your Organization.* Ask participants to bring the reading (as well as any pre-work worksheets) with them to the workshop and to be ready to discuss it.

Practical Application Exercises

Each section that explores The Five Most Important Questions ends with a Practical Application exercise that allows participants to engage in dialogue using worksheets from the *Participant Workbook.*

Each of these exercises concludes with a group discussion that asks participants to think about how to design self-assessment for their own organizations. During these discussions you will need to label a flip chart or section of a whiteboard with the question you are working with ("What is our mission?") and you will ask the group for at least five ideas on how to design the self-assessment process.

These steps will be used again during Exercise 9—"Self-Assessment—Process Design." Make sure you have enough space around the room to display steps for each question. Participants will use the information to create a more detailed self-assessment design for their organizations.

Workshop Set-Up

Arrange the tables and chairs in the room so that participants can work in their groups of three to six. Use tent cards to assign seating. When possible, ensure that the room has enough space for groups to use flip charts or whiteboards. Make sure you have all of the necessary supplies and that all equipment is working properly (see the "Supplies and Equipment Checklist" in Section 2).

At each table, make sure each participant receives a packet with the following materials:

- The program agenda

- Copies of the PowerPoint slides you will be using, with space alongside each slide to take notes

- A *Participant Workbook,* if it has not been delivered to participants prior to the workshop

- Notepad and pen

Project PowerPoint Slide 1 on the screen, so participants can see it as they enter the workshop.

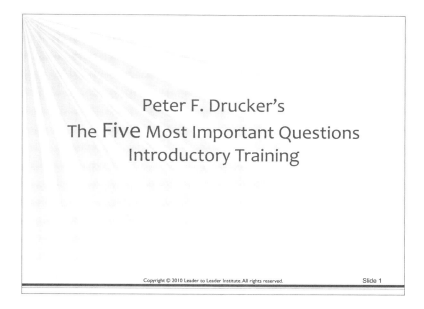

Optional: Have music playing as participants arrive—to create energy for the group. You can play music at the end of each break in the program to signal to participants that it is time to start the next workshop segment. You may also want to project inspirational imagery or photographs at this point or at other times during the workshop.

Welcome, Introductions, and Objectives

- Half-day and full-day training time: 20 minutes
- Two-day training time: 30 minutes
- Slides: 1–11

Welcome

- All workshops time: 5 minutes

Note for the introduction: *Ask the sponsor of the self-assessment training to introduce you to the participants and set the context for the workshop.*

SAY Welcome everyone! We are pleased to have the opportunity to explore The Five Most Important Questions with you.

Note for facilitators: *Make sure you present your professional background, highlighting your work and/or experience with self-assessment, strategic planning, and other related workshops.*

Note for organizational leaders: *If you are providing the training for your own organization or for your partners or members, provide some context as to why your organization is holding a workshop on self-assessment.*

Introductions

- Half-day and full-day training time: 5 minutes
- Two-day training time: 10 minutes

SAY Let's go around the room and make introductions. Please tell us who you are, your organization [*if applicable*], and your role, including title.

Note: *You do not need to ask for names, organizations, and roles if participants already know each other. If you have time, you may want to conduct a brief icebreaker to encourage sharing.*

Optional icebreaker: *Go around the room and ask participants to offer the first one or two words that come to mind when they hear the term* strategic planning. *Record the words on a flip chart or whiteboard. Once the group has finished, look for any patterns or themes. When appropriate, refer back to the icebreaker during the workshop.*

Purpose, Goals, Agenda, and Tool

- Half-day and full-day training time: 10 minutes
- Two-day training time: 15 minutes

SHOW Slide 2: Purpose

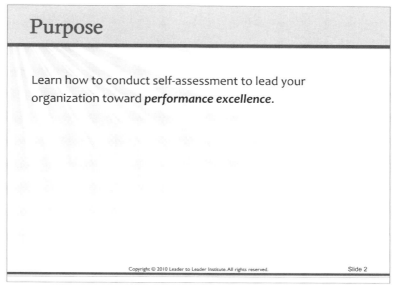

Note: Read through the slide and speak to the purpose of the workshop.

SHOW Slide 3: Goals

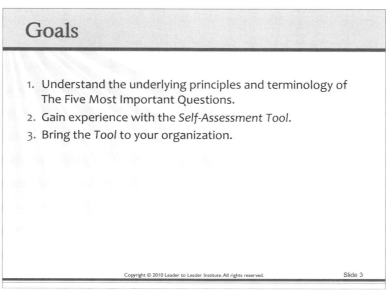

Note: Review workshop goals.

Note: For the half-day workshop, show slides 4 and 5; for the full-day session, show slides 6 and 7; for the two-day session, show slides 8, 9, and 10.

SHOW Slide 4: Half-Day Agenda

Half-Day Workshop – Agenda

• Welcome	20 min.
• **Provide Overview**	30 min.
• **Explore The Five Most Important Questions**	
What is our mission?	30 min.
• **Break**	10 min.
Who is our customer?	30 min.

Slide 4

SHOW Slide 5: Half-Day Agenda

Half-Day Workshop – Agenda (cont'd)

What does the customer value?	20 min.
What are our results?	30 min.
What is our plan?	20 min.
• **Break**	10 min.
• **Reflect on The Five Most Important Questions**	10 min.
• **Bring Self-Assessment to Your Organization**	30 min.

Slide 5

SHOW Slide 6: Full-Day Agenda

Full-Day Workshop – Agenda

- Welcome — 20 min.
- **Provide Overview** — 45 min.
- Break — 15 min.
- **Explore The Five Most Important Questions**
  What is our mission? — 60 min.
  Who is our customer? — 45 min.
- Lunch — 60 min.

Slide 6

SHOW Slide 7: Full-Day Agenda

Full-Day Workshop – Agenda (cont'd)

What does the customer value? — 45 min.
What are our results? — 45 min.
What is our plan? — 40 min.
- Break — 15 min.
- **Reflect on The Five Most Important Questions** — 30 min.
- **Bring Self-Assessment to Your Organization** — 60 min.

Slide 7

SHOW Slide 8: Two-Day Agenda

Two-Day Workshop – Day 1

• Welcome	30 min.
• **Provide Overview**	45 min.
• Break	15 min.
• **Explore The Five Most Important Questions**	
What is our mission?	90 min.
• Lunch	60 min.

Slide 8

SHOW Slide 9: Two-Day Agenda

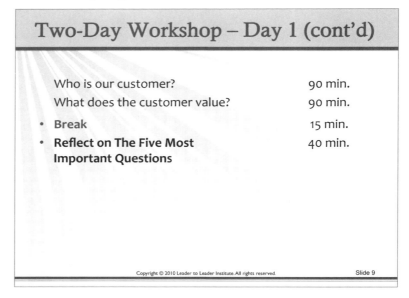

Two-Day Workshop – Day 1 (cont'd)

Who is our customer?	90 min.
What does the customer value?	90 min.
• Break	15 min.
• **Reflect on The Five Most Important Questions**	40 min.

Slide 9

SHOW Slide 10: Two-Day Agenda

Two-Day Workshop – Day 2

•	Review of Day 1	15 min.
	What are our results?	90 min.
•	Break	15 min.
	What is our plan?	60 min.
•	Lunch	60 min.
•	Reflect on The Five Most Important Questions	60 min.
•	Break	10 min.
•	Bring Self-Assessment to Your Organization	90 min.

Note: Review the agenda with participants and note the following.

SAY We are going to experience what it is like to ask The Five Most Important Questions, or conduct self-assessment.

The *Self-Assessment Tool* engages leaders in a dialogue that changes lives.

The *Tool* was developed by Peter Drucker, widely recognized as "the Father of Modern Management." We begin our workshop by taking a look at Drucker's principles and language.

Then we explore The Five Most Important Questions. As we do this, you will gain an understanding of what it is like to engage in dialogue for each question. You will have time to think about how you will design self-assessment to meet the needs of your organization.

After gaining some experience with self-assessment, you will reflect on how it has impacted your approach to strategic planning.

One of the goals of this workshop is to provide you with the basics for conducting self-assessment. We will end the workshop with an exercise that will help you bring self-assessment to your organization.

SHOW Slide 11: Self-Assessment Tool

> ## Self-Assessment Tool
>
> - *The Five Most Important Questions You Will Ever Ask About Your Organization* – Peter F. Drucker with Jim Collins, Philip Kotler, James Kouzes, Judith Rodin, V. Kasturi Rangan, and Frances Hesselbein
>
> - *Peter F. Drucker's The Five Most Important Questions Self-Assessment Tool, Facilitator's Guide, Third Edition* – Leader to Leader Institute
>
> - *The Five Most Important Questions Self-Assessment Tool, Participant Workbook, Third Edition* – Peter F. Drucker
>
>   Slide 11

SAY During the training, we will be working with all three parts of the *Self-Assessment Tool*:

1. The book *The Five Most Important Questions You Will Ever Ask About Your Organization*

2. The *Facilitator's Guide*

3. The *Participant Workbook*

You were asked to read *The Five Most Important Questions You Will Ever Ask About Your Organization* prior to the workshop.

ASK How many of you were able to do so?

Note: *Take a quick count.*

SAY During our workshop, we will draw upon this reading. You will also find the little book to be a great reference after the workshop. You can use it to refresh your memory and to keep The Five Most Important Questions at the top of your mind as you carry out your daily work.

For application purposes, this reading can be used to familiarize your organization with self-assessment. It is a good resource for bringing the *Tool* to your board's attention.

During the training, we also will be using a selection of worksheets from the *Participant Workbook*. This will allow you to experience the power of The Five Most Important Questions.

For application purposes, the *Workbook* is used to engage your organization in facilitated dialogue, which is at the heart of self-assessment.

I will be using the *Facilitator's Guide*, and after this training, you can use one to present self-assessment to your organization. Section 1 of the *Guide* offers greater detail on process design. You can use this section to adapt self-assessment to meet the needs of your organization.

ASK Are there any questions about the agenda and the *Tool*?

Note: Field questions about the agenda and workshop materials.

SAY Let's start with an overview of self-assessment.

Overview of Self-Assessment

- Half-day training time: 30 minutes

- Full-day training time: 45 minutes

- Two-day training time: 45 minutes

- Slides: 12–24

SAY First, a little bit about the leaders who have made self-assessment possible.

SHOW Slide 12: Peter F. Drucker

SAY Peter Drucker is the architect of the *Self-Assessment Tool*.

He is widely considered to be the world's foremost pioneer of management theory.

Central to his philosophy is the view that *people* are an organization's *most valuable* resource and a manager's job is to *prepare* and *free* people to perform.

He leveraged his theories on leadership and management to design the *Tool* specifically for social sector organizations.

Optional: *Ask participants if they use Peter Drucker's leadership and management wisdom in their daily practice. If yes, probe for some examples.*

SHOW   Slide 13: Frances Hesselbein

SAY   Frances Hesselbein is a pioneer for women, volunteerism, and diversity. She is an example of leadership in action. Frances Hesselbein served as CEO of the Girl Scouts of the U.S.A. from 1976 through 1990. In 1998 she was awarded the Presidential Medal of Freedom, the highest civilian honor in the United States.

With Peter Drucker, in 1990 she founded the Peter F. Drucker Foundation for Nonprofit Management, now the Leader to Leader Institute. Soon after, the *Self-Assessment Tool* was created to bring Peter Drucker's wisdom to the social sector.

Frances Hesselbein continues to serve. In 2009 the University of Pittsburgh introduced *The Hesselbein Global Academy for Student Leadership and Civic Engagement*. Also in 2009, Frances was named *Class of 1951 Chair for the Study of Leadership* at the United States Military Academy at West Point.

The Social Sector

- All workshops time: 3 minutes

SHOW Slide 14: The Social Sector

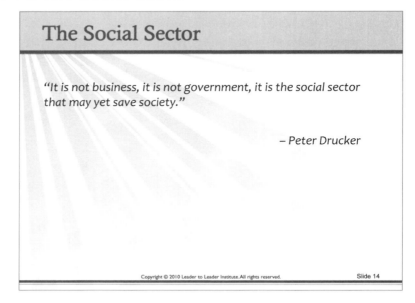

ASK The *Tool* was designed specifically for the social sector. What is the social sector? How is it different from other sectors—business and public?

Optional: If you work for a business or government agency with a socially beneficial mission, how is your organization similar to one in the social sector and how is it different?

Note: Prompt the group for two to three responses and compare with the following points.

SAY The term *social sector* was created as an alternative to *nonprofit* and *nongovernmental*, which emphasize what the sector is *not*, rather than calling attention to a focus on social mission.

Social sector organizations serve a social need. Performance is measured in the form of *changed lives*. Social sector organizations exhibit the following characteristics:

- They are mission-driven.
- They are results-oriented (measured in changed lives).

- Operations and funding are dedicated to serve a social need.

Exercise 1: Performance Excellence

Purpose

- To visualize performance excellence

Time

Full-day and two-day training: 12 minutes

Note: *This exercise could be skipped if conducting a half-day workshop or if you would like to spend more time during the full-day and two-day workshops on the other group exercises.*

SAY Now for a short exercise. Our theme today is "performance excellence" and the courageous leadership necessary to achieve it.[15]

Please think about a time when you experienced performance excellence.

- What did it feel like?
- What were its characteristics?

Visualize as many details as possible. Please take a minute in silence. Write your thoughts down if you would like.

Note: *Allow a minute of silence and then ask participants to form small groups of two or three.*

SAY Now, please form small groups of two or three and talk about your experience with performance excellence. Come up with two to three key phrases to describe what performance excellence means. We'll stop in about five minutes— so make sure everyone has a chance to speak.

Note: *Groups do not need to be the same as the groups selected for Practical Application exercises. After about five minutes, bring the discussion back to the whole group.*

ASK Who would like to offer his or her insight into what performance excellence means? What did your group discuss?

Note: Prompt for three to five responses and compare these with the points shown on slide 15. Hold discussion for the remainder of the exercise.

SHOW Slide 15: Performance Excellence

Performance Excellence

- Manage for the mission
- Focus on the customer and results
- Embrace diversity
- Share responsibility and accountability
- Innovate
- Make course corrections

Slide 15

Note: Write any additional thoughts from participants on performance excellence on a flip chart. Refer to this exercise whenever appropriate during the workshop.

About Self-Assessment, Drucker's Terms

- Half-day training time: 25 minutes

- Full-day and two-day training time: 30 minutes

Note: For the half-day session, you'll need to move through this section very quickly; however, it is important that you introduce all of Drucker's terms.

SAY Let's now talk about the *Self-Assessment Tool*. What is it?

- Self-assessment goes to the heart of an organization: why it exists and what it must do to make a difference.
- The *Tool* is a strategic thinking process.
- It is a framework of powerfully simple questions designed to keep organizations focused on results.

SAY The *Tool* suits the needs of social sector organizations because

- It is *flexible* and *can be adapted* to meet a variety of planning and leadership needs.
- It is easy to learn and use.
- It does not require a significant amount of training to implement.
- It brings a minimal amount of disruption to operations.

SAY Why is the *Tool* used?

SHOW Slide 16: The *Tool* is used to

> ## The *Tool* is used to
>
> - Deepen understanding of the mission
> - Conduct organizational strategic planning
> - Listen to the customer
> - Define results
> - Clarify organizational goals
> - Plan to achieve results
>
> Copyright © 2010 Leader to Leader Institute. All rights reserved.   Slide 16

Note: Review the points on the slide.

ASK Are there any questions about why self-assessment is used?

Note: The participants will be gaining a better understanding of why the Tool is used during the workshop. More detailed questions about "why" can be reserved for more appropriate sections of the workshop.

Organizational Self-Assessment

Note: It is important to cover this section of the overview. You will come back to it for the final segment of the workshop, "Bring Self-Assessment to Your Organization." To prepare for this section, refer to Section 1.

SAY Now let's talk a little bit about how self-assessment is conducted and what it requires.

SHOW Slide 17: Organizational Self-Assessment

Organizational Self-Assessment

- Gain commitment from leadership
- Design self-assessment
- Conduct self-assessment
- Take action: determine direction, prepare, approve, and implement plan

Slide 17

SAY This training focuses on *organizational self-assessment*— strategic planning for the total organization. The four major components of designing self-assessment are

- Gain commitment
- Design
- Conduct
- Take action

Gain Commitment

SAY Organizational self-assessment requires commitment from the board and the management team.

ASK What are the responsibilities of the board and management team?

Note: Take three to five responses and compare these with the following points.

SAY The board is responsible for

- The strategic plan (vision, mission, and goals)
- Performance appraisal and oversight

Note: "Appraisal and oversight" includes reviewing annual and interim management reports, ensuring the organization's legal compliance and standards of practice, and maintaining fiduciary responsibility for the organization.

SAY Management is responsible for

- Operational or tactical planning (objectives, action steps, and budget)
- Performance

ASK Who leads self-assessment?

Note: Take one or two responses.

SAY The board chairman and the chief executive officer lead organizational self-assessment.

The chairman recommends to the board that self-assessment be undertaken.[16] Once self-assessment has been conducted, the chairman brings the plan before the board for approval.

The CEO coordinates self-assessment and ensures that the organization reaches the desired outcomes as directed by the board. Once the mission and goals of the organization have been approved by the board, the CEO develops the operational plan with input from the board and staff. The chairman then brings the operational plan before the board for approval.

Design

SAY Organizational self-assessment takes about three to six months to conduct.

The design details the steps your organization will take to conduct self-assessment, starting with introducing self-assessment to the board and ending with implementing and appraising the plan. It outlines who is responsible for what tasks and by when.

The design must support your organization's purpose for undertaking self-assessment as well as what the board and management team expect to gain from the process.

As part of the design, you will form a Self-Assessment Team, which includes those leading and managing the effort as well as those participating in facilitated dialogue and organizational planning. You will select a facilitator and design dialogue sessions. You will include any data gathering and analysis requirements into your design. We will discuss the types of data that inform self-assessment as we move through the workshop.

Conduct

SAY   When you are ready to conduct self-assessment, engage your organization's leaders in dialogue and inform that dialogue with data. It is essential to use a facilitator (from inside or outside the organization) to prepare and engage the Self-Assessment Team in dialogue. The facilitator must have experience with The Five Most Important Questions or strategic planning.

Take Action

SAY   The major findings, decisions, and recommendations generated during dialogue are used by your board and management team for planning. First, the board develops and approves the strategic plan—it revisits the mission and sets the goals.

Once the mission and goals have been approved by the board, the CEO develops the objectives, action steps, and budget. As soon as the board approves the operational plan, the organization must take action.

Implementing the plan involves communicating the plan, preparing the organization for strategic and operational change, and appraising performance.

Note: Use Section 1 of the Facilitator's Guide *to offer additional thoughts and insights to process.*

ASK   Are there any questions about how self-assessment is conducted?

Note: The participants will be gaining a better understanding of how the Tool *is used during the training. More detailed questions about "how" can be reserved for more appropriate sections of the training.*

Terminology

> **Note:** *While you are talking through this section, show slides 18, 19, and 20 so participants can see Drucker's terms.*

SAY   The *Tool* uses Peter Drucker's leadership and management terminology.

A glossary of terms can be found in the *Participant Workbook* on p. 99.

SHOW   Slides 18, 19, and 20: Drucker's Core Terms

Drucker's Core Terms

- Action steps
- Appraisal
- Budget
- Concentration
- Constructive dissent
- Customer (primary and supporting)
- Customer value

Slide 18

Drucker's Core Terms (cont'd)

- Depth interviews
- Environmental scan
- Goals
- Innovation
- Internal data
- Leadership team
- Mission

Slide 19

Drucker's Core Terms (cont'd)

- Objectives
- Plan
- Planned abandonment
- Qualitative measures
- Quantitative measures
- Results
- Trend
- Vision

Slide 20

SAY It is essential to use Drucker's terms while engaging the organization in self-assessment.

For our purposes, let's agree to use Drucker's language.

ASK Is everyone on board with using the language of the *Tool*?

Note: Be aware of any immediate struggle with or opposition to the terms. Emphasize that Drucker carefully selected the terms to keep organizations focused on performance. Participants will have the opportunity to discover why during the workshop.

SAY I will be defining terms as they are introduced in the workshop, but let's take a look at three before we start learning about The Five Most Important Questions.

SHOW Slide 21: Constructive Dissent

Constructive Dissent

Using dissent or disagreement as an opportunity to "[create] understanding and mutual respect"

Note: The slide will be blank and will require a "click" to populate the definition. Initiate the discussion first. Once the group has had a chance to think about the term, then bring up the definition.

ASK   What do you think this term means?

Note: Ask for three or four suggestions and then compare these with the narrative below. Click on the slide to bring up and review the definition.

SAY   Decision making in self-assessment often involves risk.

At times, dissent or disagreement emerges.

Drucker asks us to be open to dissent, to make it constructive.

ASK   Can anyone offer an example of when dissent or disagreement helped your organization make a decision?

Note: Ask for one or two accounts.

ASK   What are some ways to encourage constructive dissent during self-assessment?

Note: Ask for two to three suggestions and compare with the points below.

SAY   Those leading self-assessment, likely the board chairman and the CEO, need to encourage and be open to constructive dissent throughout self-assessment.

A skillful, unbiased facilitator is essential to the self-assessment process and in helping leaders use constructive dissent to work through conflict.

In *Managing the Nonprofit Organization*, Drucker offers guidelines for using constructive dissent. He says

- Ensure that each person or faction has the opportunity to speak.
- Assume that each person or faction has the right answer, but make sure everyone is clear about what question each person or faction is trying to answer.
- Never ask who is right or what is right.[17]

SHOW   Slide 22: Customer

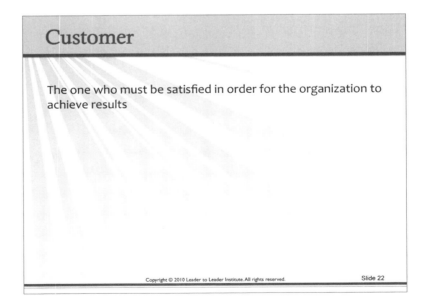

Note: The slide will be blank and will require a "click" to populate the definition. Initiate the discussion first. Once the group has had a chance to think about the term, then bring up the definition.

SAY Next, let's take a look at "Customer."

ASK What do you think the definition for "Customer" is?

Note: Ask for one or two thoughts and then click on the slide to bring up and review the definition.

"Customer" will be defined further during the segment on "Who Is Our Customer?" You can defer any lengthy discussion on "customer" until that segment.

SHOW Slide 23: Results

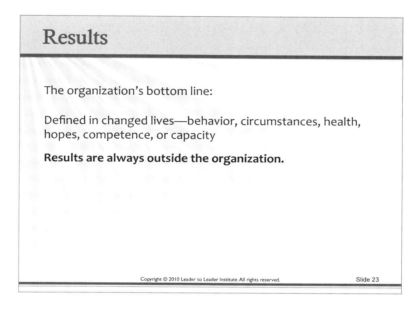

Note: The slide will be blank and will require a "click" to populate the definition. Initiate the discussion first. Once the group has had a chance to think about the term, then bring up the definition.

ASK How about results—what do you think Drucker's definition for "results" is?

Note: Ask for one or two thoughts and then click on the slide to bring up and review the definition.

"Results" will be defined further during the segment on "What Are Our Results?" You can defer any lengthy discussion on "results" until that segment.

SAY Throughout the workshop, keep thinking about the relationship between "Customer" and "Results."

SHOW Slide 24: Ground Rules

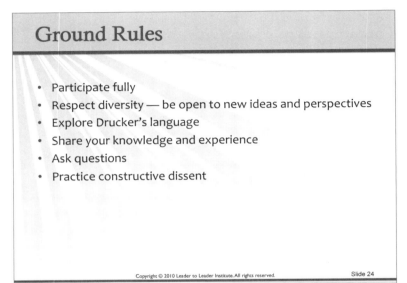

Slide 24

Within slide:

Ground Rules

- Participate fully
- Respect diversity — be open to new ideas and perspectives
- Explore Drucker's language
- Share your knowledge and experience
- Ask questions
- Practice constructive dissent

SAY Finally, let's set some ground rules.

ASK Would anyone like to add anything? Do we have agreement on the ground rules?

Note: Review the points on the slide. Field any new ground rules from the group. Place them on a flip chart and refer back to the ground rules whenever necessary throughout the workshop.

What Is Our Mission?

Half-Day Training Time: 30 minutes

Time Breakdown (approximation)

- 5 minutes for Exercise 2: What Is Our Mission?

- 10 minutes to present principles and terminology

- 15 minutes for Exercise 3: Practical Application: Look Outside the Window

Full-Day Training Time: 60 minutes

Time Breakdown (approximation)

- 15 minutes for Exercise 2: What Is Our Mission?

- 15 minutes to present principles and terminology

- 30 minutes for Exercise 3: Practical Application—Look Outside the Window

Two-Day Training Time: 90 minutes

Time Breakdown (approximation)

- 20 minutes for Exercise 2: What Is Our Mission?

- 20 minutes to present principles and terminology

- 50 minutes for Exercise 3: Practical Application—Look Outside the Window

Slides: 25–36

Focus Points

The effective mission

- Is sharp, focused, and clear; is easily understood and remembered

- Defines purpose—an organization's reason for being

- Inspires and motivates people to action

- Preserves the core, yet stimulates progress (Jim Collins)

Related Worksheets in *Participant Workbook*

*Worksheet 1.1: What Is Our Current Mission?

Worksheet 1.2: Does Our Mission Need to Be Revisited?

*Worksheet 1.3: What Are the Emerging Trends That Will Have the Greatest Impact?

Worksheet 1.4: What Are Our Opportunities?

(*used as part of group work during the training session)

SHOW   Slide 25: What Is Our Mission?

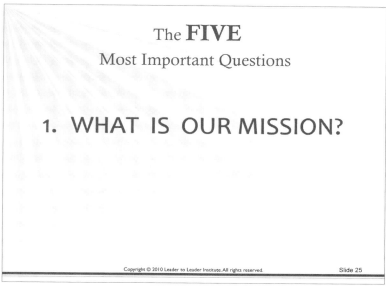

The **FIVE**
Most Important Questions

1. WHAT IS OUR MISSION?

Slide 25

SAY   To start exploring The Five Most Important Questions, let's start with a small-group exercise, which will help us begin thinking about "Mission."

Exercise 2: What Is Our Mission?

Purpose

- For participants to start thinking about "Mission"

Time

Half-day training: 5 minutes

Full-day training: 15 minutes

Two-day training: 20 minutes

Worksheets

Worksheets 1.1 and 1.2

Instructions

Full-day: Participants will use Worksheet 1.1 to explore mission. They will complete the worksheet individually first, and then work in groups of two to three to discuss their mission, as well as their experience exploring mission. Groups do not need to be the same as the groups that are selected for the Practical Application exercises. You will end this exercise by holding a full-group discussion. Estimated time is as follows:

- 3 minutes: participants complete Worksheet 1.1.
- 5 to 6 minutes: pairs discuss mission, and so on.
- 5 to 6 minutes: participants have large-group discussion.

Two-day: Participants will work through the full-day exercise, but will also complete Worksheet 1.2 before working in groups of two or three. Groups will share their mission and then discuss their experience exploring "Mission." Estimated time is as follows:

- 2 minutes: participants complete Worksheet 1.1.
- 3 minutes: participants complete Worksheet 1.2.
- 8 to 10 minutes: pairs discuss mission, and so on.
- 5 to 7 minutes: participants have large-group discussion.

Half-day: In a half-day session, the goal will simply be to introduce Worksheet 1.1 and allow participants a few minutes to familiarize themselves with it. Working as a full group, you should review Worksheet 1.1 and allow a few minutes for group responses and discussion. You'll need to adjust the following script accordingly.

SAY You are going to use Worksheet 1.1 to think about your mission.

I would like you to spend a few minutes completing Questions (a), (b), and (c) on your own, and then you'll work in small groups to discuss what it is like to explore "Mission."

***Note:** (For two-day workshops, introduce Worksheet 1.2 alongside Worksheet 1.1.) Make sure participants understand how to use the worksheet(s). If participants struggle with the worksheet(s), ask them to think about what information they need to truly explore "Mission." After participants have used the worksheet(s), ask them to form groups of two to three.*

SAY Now form groups of two to three and discuss your mission and what it was like to explore it. Then we will discuss our findings with the entire group.

> *Note: After the appropriate length of time (5 to 6 minutes for the full-day session; 8 to 10 minutes for the two-day session), move participants back to a full-group discussion.*

ASK What did you experience when you started to work with "Mission"?

> *Note: Ask for two or three insights and experiences. Probe to see if anything was illuminating or challenging about this initial exploration of mission.*

ASK Who feels "Mission" needs to be revisited?

> *Note: Ask for a show of hands—you should ask this question and track how the response changes during the workshop as participants explore The Five Most Important Questions. For participants who feel they need to revisit their Mission, probe for why.*

SAY Keep "Mission" in mind as you explore Drucker's questions. During self-assessment you will often come back to mission to see whether or not it requires revision.

Principles and Terminology

- *Half-day training time:* 10 minutes
- *Full-day training time:* 18 minutes
- *Two-day training time:* 20 minutes

> *Note: For the half-day workshop, you'll need to go through the terms quickly and likely won't have time to ask or take questions.*

SAY Let's now discuss some of the principles and terms for "Mission."

ASK Why is it important to think about mission? How would you define mission?

> *Note: Ask for two or three thoughts.*

SHOW Slide 26: Mission Defined

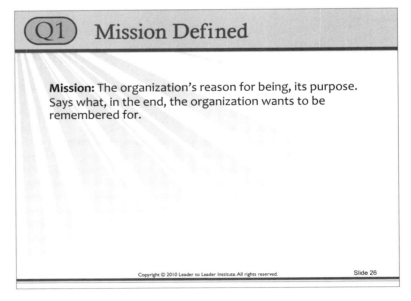

Note: Review definition of mission.

SAY Here is what Drucker says about mission.

SHOW Slides 27 and 28: Drucker on Mission[18]

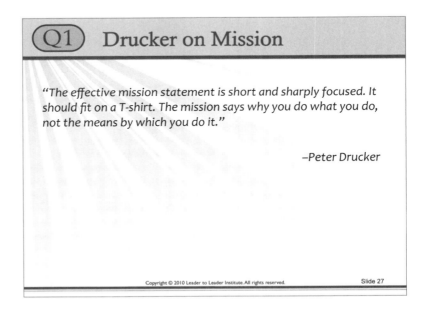

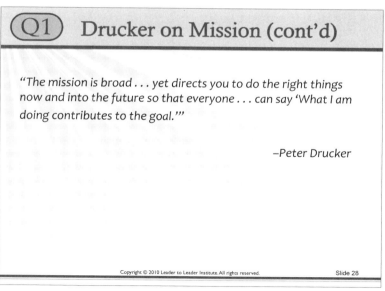

Note: Read through the slides.

ASK   What are Drucker's key points?

Note: Ask for five or six points and write them on a flip chart. Compare them to the four teaching points on the following slides (the mission conveys focus, purpose, inspiration, and preservation of the core).

SHOW   Slide 29: Is Focused

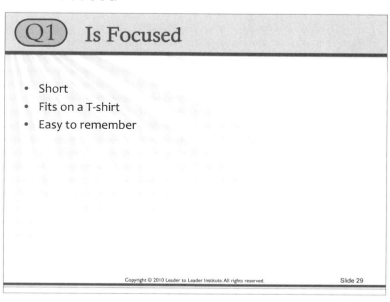

SAY   The mission is short and focused. Drucker says it should "fit on a T-shirt."

Anyone who hears or reads the mission can understand what it means.

The mission is easy to remember.

SHOW   Slide 30: Defines Purpose

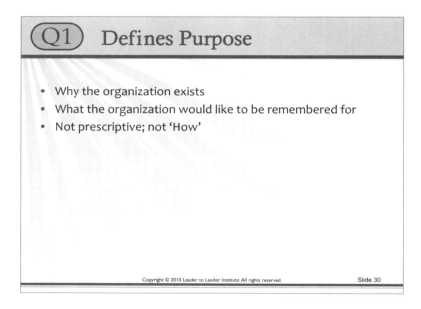

SAY   The mission defines purpose—the organization's reason for being.

It does *not* prescribe means—*how*, *what*, or *when* things are done.

SHOW Slide 31: Inspires

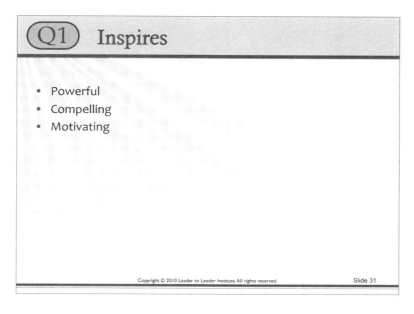

SAY The mission inspires. It compels the organization to action and motivates it to achieve results.

SAY Here is Jim Collins on mission.

SHOW Slide 32: Collins on Mission[19]

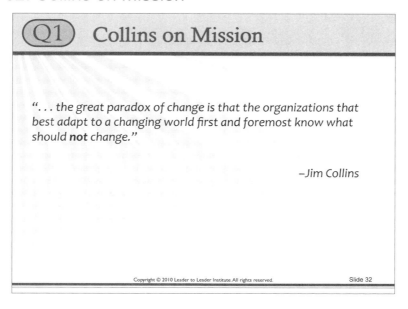

SAY What are your thoughts about what Collins is saying?

Note: Ask for two to three comments and compare these with the following points.

SAY For Collins, mission reminds us to preserve the core, but stimulate progress.

Core means values and fundamental purpose, while *progress* means change, improvement, innovation, and renewal.

ASK How does the organization define its mission?

Note: Draw three to four responses from the group.

SAY You first "look outside the window." You must look at the external environment. Drucker says,

"The organization that starts from the inside and then tries to find places to put its resources is going to fritter itself away. Above all, it will focus on yesterday. Demographics change. Needs change."*

ASK How does the organization "look outside the window"?

SAY It conducts an environmental scan.

ASK Who can describe what an environmental scan is?

Note: Ask for one to two responses. Ask if anyone has recently conducted an environmental scan. If yes, probe to see how the scan was conducted and how the organization benefited from it.

*Stern, Gary. *The Drucker Foundation Self-Assessment Tool Process Guide*. San Francisco: Jossey-Bass, 1999, p.15.

SHOW Slides 33 and 34: Environmental Scan and Trend[20]

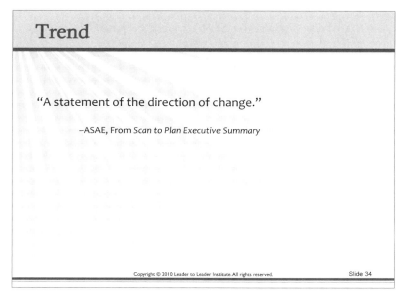

Note: *Review definitions of environmental scan and trend.*

Exercise 3: Practical Application— Look Outside the Window

Purposes

- To identify the emerging trends that will have the greatest impact on the organization

- To prepare the organization to explore "Mission"

- *(for Two-Day only)* To look at external trends and identify the most promising opportunities for the organization

Time

Half-day training: 15 minutes

Full-day training: 30 minutes (10 for organizing groups and delivering instructions, 12 for emerging trends, 8 for large-group discussion)

Two-day training: 50 minutes (10 for organizing groups and delivering instructions, 15 for emerging trends, 15 for opportunities, 10 for large-group discussion)

Worksheet(s)

Half-day and full-day training: Worksheet 1.3

Two-day training: Worksheets 1.3 and 1.4

Note about Practical Application exercises: Each of The Five Most Important Questions in the workshop will end with a Practical Application exercise for participants to apply their knowledge of self-assessment to a real organization.

As this is the first Practical Application exercise, make participants aware of what the Practical Application exercises are, as well as the group assignments—groups will be working together for the remainder of the workshop.

If groups comprise a mix of organizations, ask the participants to select one organization to focus on. Make sure each group is comfortable with this.

As participants engage in the Practical Application exercises, they should wear two "hats." First, they should participate and observe from the perspective of someone who has been selected by the organization to participate in self-assessment.

Second, they should take turns facilitating the group. Ask them to pay close attention to group process and how the group makes decisions.

At the end of each Practical Application you will hold a large-group discussion. Participants will reflect on their group work and recommend at least five steps to prepare the organization for self-assessment. Record the steps on flip charts.

You will collect process-related steps at the end of each Practical Application exercise. You will display these steps during the final exercise, "Self-Assessment—Process Design," for participants to refer to as they create a more detailed self-assessment design for their organization. Make sure you will be able to display the steps where all the groups can see them.

During group work, observe groups and reinforce or clarify major focus points and terminology.

Instructions

Half-day: Again, the point will be to introduce the concepts and related worksheet. Working as a full group, review and discuss Worksheet 1.3. Adjust the script as needed.

Full-day: Groups will use Worksheet 1.3, Questions (a) and (b). They will use Question a to identify emerging trends that will have an impact on the organization. They will use Question (b) to identify the *three* trends that will have the greatest impact on the organization. Note that Question (b) has space for five trends, so instruct groups that they only need to think of three. They can explore more if time allows.

Two-day: Groups will follow the instructions above, as well as use Worksheet 1.4, Questions (a) and (b). The table in Question (a) is used to identify opportunities for the organization. Groups will use Question (b) to review the opportunities listed in Question (a) and decide which are the most promising. They should identify two or three. You can introduce Worksheet 1.4 once groups have finished Worksheet 1.3. Take the following steps to move through the exercise:

1. Introduce the Practical Application exercises. Indicate that they will occur at the end of each question and provide the opportunity for participants to apply what they have learned to a real organization.

2. Make participants aware of their group assignments. Bring attention to the group composition (it should be diverse). It will be important for participants to reflect on what it is like to conduct self-assessment with a diverse set of leaders.

3. If groups comprise leaders from multiple organizations, ask them to select one organization on which to focus.

4. Ask participants to wear two "hats"—one of an organizational leader who has been asked to participate in self-assessment, the other of a facilitator who has been asked to guide dialogue. Ask the members of each group to take turns facilitating. As they do, ask them to focus on "process"—how the group is communicating and making decisions.

5. Indicate that the exercise will end in a large-group discussion, during which participants can explore how they will apply what they have learned to their organization.

6. Deliver instructions for the exercise; make sure groups understand them and know how to use the worksheet(s).

7. For this exercise, groups should spend the first one or two minutes reviewing the organization's mission.

8. If groups have difficulty identifying trends, ask them to think about what information they need to gather to identify trends.

9. If flip charts are available, let groups know they can use them to facilitate dialogue and record major findings and decisions.

10. Provide groups time warnings to ensure that they complete the exercise. Stop at the prescribed time and bring participants back into a large-group discussion.

ASK Who would like to share his or her group's trends?

Note: Ask two to three different groups to share emerging trends.

ASK How did it feel to "look outside the window"? How did you decide on your trends? Was there any discussion? Was there any need for further analysis?

Note: Ask for two to three responses and probe for more detail when appropriate.

ASK (for two-day only) Who would like to share the organization's most promising opportunities?

Note: Ask for two to three responses and probe for more detail when appropriate. You can use questions similar to the ones above. (Was there any debate? Was there any need for further analysis?)

ASK Now let's talk about process. What was it like to participate in a dialogue on "Mission"? What was it like to facilitate?

Note: Ask for two responses from the participants' point of view and two responses from the facilitators' point of view.

ASK What insights did you gain? What is needed for a productive dialogue on "Mission"? What steps will you take to prepare your organization for a dialogue on "Mission"?

*Note: Label a flip chart "Mission." Work with the group to identify at least **five** steps and write them on the flip chart. Ask participants to set aside some pages in their notebooks to track design steps for "Mission" and each of the other questions. To focus the group on process, you might ask*

- *Who in your organization will you ask to participate in a dialogue on "Mission"?* (The board must be engaged in the dialogue.)

- *What data will you need to gather and analyze to inform a dialogue on "Mission"?* (environmental scan)

- *What qualities in a facilitator will you seek?*

- *How much time will you reserve for a dialogue on "Mission"? What will the venue look like?*

- *What do you think will be the outcomes of a dialogue on "Mission"?*

SHOW Slide 35: Practical Application

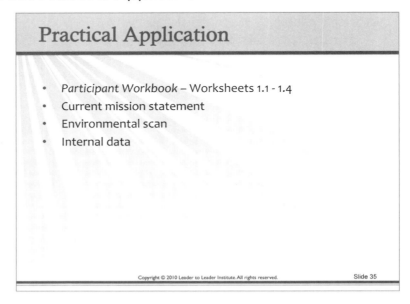

SAY Remember there are additional worksheets on "Mission" in the *Participant Workbook*. Worksheet 1.2 asks you to rate your current mission. Worksheet 1.4 asks you to use external trends to identify the most promising opportunities for the organization.

Note: You do not need to mention Worksheet 1.2 or 1.4 if you are conducting the two-day workshop.

When preparing your organization for self-assessment, it will be important for you to familiarize yourself with these worksheets, as well as the other resources listed here.

Internal Data are summarized information regarding your organization's history, present status, and performance.

SHOW Slide 36: Question 1: Focus Points

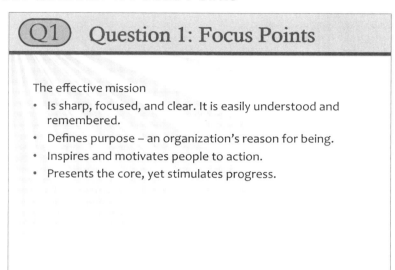

ASK These are the major points we have covered. Are there any questions or comments before we move to Question 2?

Who Is Our Customer?

Half-Day Training Time: 30 minutes

Time Breakdown (approximation)

- 10 minutes to present principles and terminology

- 20 minutes for Exercise 4: Practical Application—Who Is Our Customer?

Full-Day Training Time: 45 minutes

Time Breakdown (approximation)

- 15 minutes to present principles and terminology

- 30 minutes for Exercise 4: Practical Application—Who Is Our Customer?

Two-Day Training Time: 90 minutes

Time Breakdown (approximation)

- 30 minutes to present principles and terminology

- 60 minutes for Exercise 4: Practical Application—Who Is Our Customer?

Slides: 37–46

Focus Points

- The customer is at the heart of self-assessment

- The customer is the person who must be satisfied in order for the organization to achieve results

- The primary customer is the person whose life is changed through the organization's work

- Supporting customers are those who, in addition to the primary customer, must be satisfied for the organization to achieve results

- An organization has one primary customer; it may have multiple supporting customers

- The customer can accept or reject what the organization has to offer

Related Worksheets in *Participant Workbook*

*Worksheet 2.1: Who Are Our Primary and Supporting Customers?

*Worksheet 2.2: How Will Our Customers Change?

Worksheet 2.3: Are We Serving the Right Customers?

(*used as part of the small-group work at the end of the session)

Note: *For both the half- and full-day sessions, you'll need to focus on presenting the material and limit questions and discussion.*

SHOW Slide 37: Who Is Our Customer?

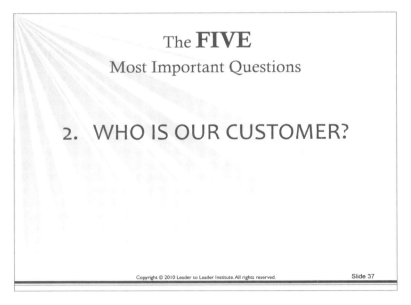

SAY The next two questions, 2 and 3, focus on the "customer."

SHOW Slide 38: Drucker on Customer[21]

SAY Drucker asks,

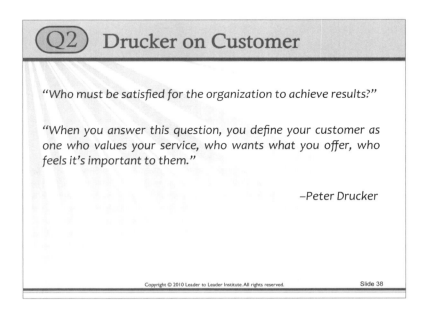

Note: Review slide.

SHOW   Slide 39: The Customer Is Key

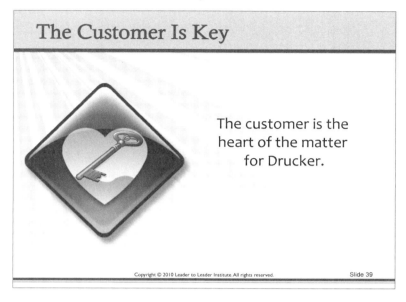

SAY   The *customer* is at the heart of the *Tool*. In self-assessment, *Who is our customer?* and *What does the customer value?* are used to identify and listen to the customer.

These two questions help organizations challenge assumptions and focus on results, so that they can change lives.

SHOW   Slide 40: Customer Defined

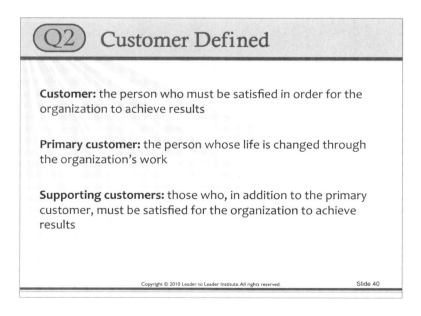

SAY Customers need to be *satisfied*. They can accept or reject what the organization has to offer. Self-assessment breaks customers into two groups: primary and supporting.

An organization has one primary customer. It may have multiple supporting customers.

ASK Are there any questions about how customer is defined?

Note: Field any questions and move participants into the next exercise. For half-day and full-day sessions, you might omit this exercise, in which case you'd move on to Slide 42.

SHOW Slide 41: Exercise: Girl Scouts

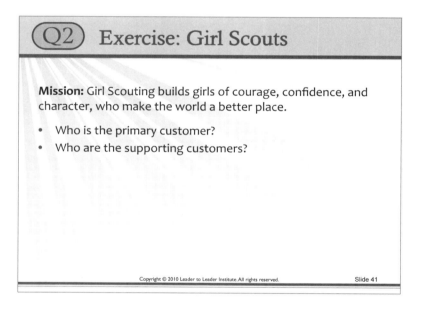

ASK This is the Girl Scouts' mission. Who is the primary customer?

*Note: Emphasize there is only **one primary customer.** Note that the primary customer might be broken into segments.*

For instance, the primary customer for the Girl Scouts is "girls." Segments are Daisies, Brownies, Juniors, Cadets, Seniors, and Ambassadors.

ASK What are the advantages of working with *one* primary customer?

Note: Ask for two to three thoughts and compare these with the point below.

SAY   One primary customer helps organizations focus on allocating limited resources to achieve results.

ASK   Who are the supporting customers for the Girl Scouts?

Note: Draw out different supporting customers. They may include volunteers, members, partners, funders, referral sources, and staff.

ASK   How does the Girl Scouts satisfy these supporting customers?

Note: Work through two of the supporting customers the group has identified. Supporting customers might be satisfied through volunteering and contributing monetarily toward results they believe in, such as meeting a community need, and so on.

SHOW   Slide 42: Kotler on Customer[22]

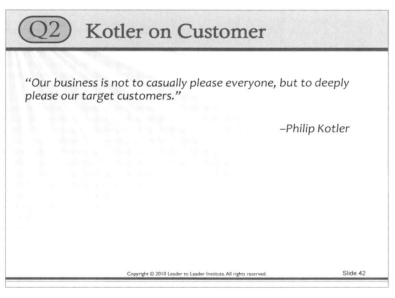

ASK   Do you agree with Philip Kotler's statement?

Note: Draw out two to three responses.

ASK   How do customers change? How are your customers changing?

Note: Draw two to three responses—probe for the participants' personal experiences. Focus participants on how the customer changes (such as number, demographics, and so on, as well as what the customer values).

SAY Drucker notes that customers are always changing.

SHOW Slides 43 and 44: Customers Change[23]

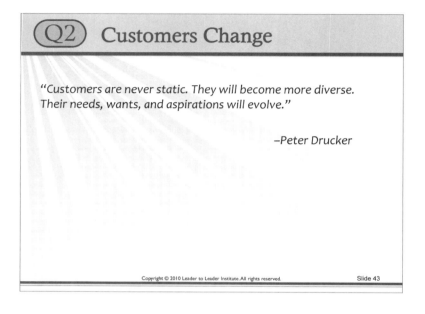

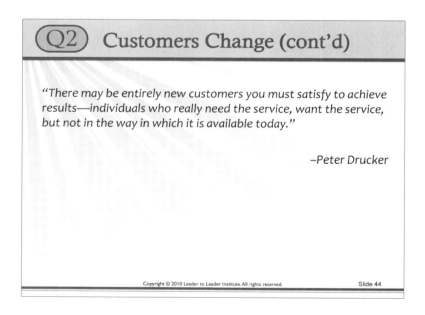

SAY Note that the organization might serve new customers over time—and it might stop serving existing customers.

Note: Probe participants for one or two personal accounts.

Exercise 4: Practical Application— Who Is Our Customer?

Purposes

- To identify the organization's customer
- To discuss how the customer is changing or may change
- To prepare the organization to explore "Customer"

Time

Half-day training: 20 minutes (5 for delivering instructions, 10 for small-group work, 5 for large-group discussion)

Full-day training: 30 minutes (5 for delivering instructions, 15 for small-group work, 10 for large-group discussion)

Two-day training: 60 minutes (5 to deliver instructions, 15 for groups to work on *primary customer,* 20 for groups to work on *supporting customers,* 20 for large-group discussion)

Worksheet(s)

Worksheets 2.1 and 2.2

Note: *Participants will work in the same groups they formed during the Practical Application exercise for "Mission." (See the note on Practical Application exercises found in Exercise 3.)*

Instructions

Half-day and Full-day: Groups will use Worksheet 2.1, Question (a), and Worksheet 2.2, Questions (a) and (b). They will use Worksheet 2.1 to identify the primary customer for the organization. They will use Worksheet 2.2, Question (a), to explore how the primary customer will change in the next three to five years. They will use Question (b) of the same worksheet to determine the impact these changes will have on the organization.

Two-Day: Groups will follow the instructions above. Once they have discussed the primary customer, they can use the same worksheets to discuss the organization's *supporting customers.* They will use

Worksheet 2.1, Question (b), to identify three to five supporting customers. The groups will select one supporting customer and use Worksheet 2.2, Questions (c) and (d), to explore how the supporting customer will change in the next three to five years and to determine the impact these changes will have on the organization. You can introduce instructions for *supporting customer* once groups have finished exploring the primary customer.

Take the following steps to move through the exercise:

1. Remind participants to continue wearing two "hats"—one as a participant in dialogue, the other as facilitator. Ask them to take turns facilitating group dialogue. As they do they should focus on group "process"—how the group is communicating and making decisions.

2. If necessary, remind groups that the exercise will end in a large-group discussion, during which participants can explore how they will apply what they have learned during the exercise to their organization.

3. Deliver instructions for the exercise; make sure groups understand the exercise and know how to use the worksheet(s).

4. If groups have difficulty identifying the customer, refer them to pages 29 and 30 of the *Participant Workbook*, "Identify the Primary Customer" and "Identify Supporting Customers." Ask groups to think about what information they need to gather to identify their customers, as well as to understand how their customers are changing.

5. Provide groups time warnings to ensure that they complete the exercise. Stop groups at the prescribed time and bring them back into a large-group discussion.

ASK Who is your primary customer?

Note: Ask two to three groups to share who their primary customer is.

ASK How did your groups decide who the primary customer is? Was there any discussion? Was there any need for further analysis?

Note: Ask for two to three responses and probe for more detail when appropriate.

ASK How will the primary customer change?

Note: Ask for two to three responses and probe for more detail when appropriate.

ASK How will the change(s) affect the organization?

ASK (for two-day only) Who are your supporting customers?

Note: Ask two to three groups to share who their supporting customers are.

ASK (for two-day only) How did your groups decide who the supporting customers are? Was there any discussion? Was there any need for further analysis?

Note: Ask two to three responses and probe for more detail when appropriate.

ASK (for two-day only) How will your supporting customer change?

Note: Ask two to three responses and probe for more detail when appropriate.

ASK How will the change(s) affect the organization?

Now let's talk about process. What was it like to participate in dialogue on "Customer"? What was it like to facilitate?

Note: Ask for two responses from the participants' point of view and two responses from the facilitators' point of view. If conducting a two-day session, instruct participants to think about both primary and supporting customers.

ASK What insights did you gain? What is needed for a productive dialogue on "Customer"? What steps will you take to prepare your organization for a dialogue on "Customer"?

*Note: Label a flip chart "Customer." Work with the group to identify at least **five** steps and write them on the flip chart. Ask participants to set aside some pages in their notebooks to track design steps for "Customer." To focus the group on process, you might ask*

- *Who in your organization will you ask to participate in a dialogue on "Customer"?* (The board must be engaged in the dialogue; also supporting customers, such as staff and volunteers, who work closely with the primary customer. Research experts. The organization may also engage the primary customer directly in dialogue.)

- *What data will you gather and analyze to inform a dialogue on "Customer"?* (environmental scan and customer research)

- *What qualities in a facilitator will you seek?*

- *How much time will you reserve for a dialogue on "Customer"? What will the venue look like?*

- *What do you think will be the outcomes of the dialogue on "Customer"?*

SHOW Slide 45: Practical Application

Practical Application

- *Participant Workbook* – Worksheets 2.1 - 2.3
- Environmental scan
- Customer research
- Internal data

Slide 45

SAY Remember there is an additional worksheet on "Customer" in the *Participant Workbook*. Worksheet 2.3 asks if you are serving the right customers.

When preparing your organization for self-assessment, it will be important for you to familiarize yourself with all the worksheets, as well as the other resources listed here.

SHOW Slide 46: Question 2: Focus Points

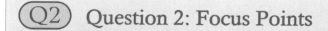

> **(Q2) Question 2: Focus Points**
>
> - The customer is at the heart of self-assessment
> - **Customer:** the person who must be satisfied in order for the organization to achieve results
> - **Primary customer:** the person whose life is changed through the organization's work (only one)
> - **Supporting customers:** those who, in addition to the primary customer, must be satisfied for the organization to achieve results (may be *multiple* in number)
> - The customer can accept or reject what the organization has to offer
>
>   Slide 46

ASK Here are the major points we have covered. Are there any questions before we move on to Question 3?

What Does the Customer Value?

Half-Day Training Time: 20 minutes
Time Breakdown (approximation)

- 10 minutes to present principles and terminology
- 10 minutes for Exercise 5: Practical Application—What Does the Customer Value?

Full-Day Training Time: 45 minutes
Time Breakdown (approximation)

- 15 minutes to present principles and terminology
- 30 minutes for Exercise 5: Practical Application—What Does the Customer Value?

Two-Day Training Time: 90 minutes
Time Breakdown (approximation)

- 30 minutes to present principles and terminology
- 60 minutes for Exercise 5: Practical Application—What Does the Customer Value?

Slides: 47–54

Focus Points

- For Drucker, "What does the customer value?" may be the most important question an organization can ask
- Customer value is that which satisfies needs, wants, and aspirations
- The organization must be committed to listening to the customer

Related Worksheets in *Participant Workbook:*

*Worksheet 3.1: What Do Our Customers Value?

Worksheet 3.2: What Knowledge Do We Need to Gain from Our Customers?

Worksheet 3.3: How Will We Gather Information?

(*used as part of the small-group work at the end of the session)

Note: *For the half-day and full-day sessions, you'll need to limit questions and discussion.*

SHOW   Slide 47: What Does the Customer Value?

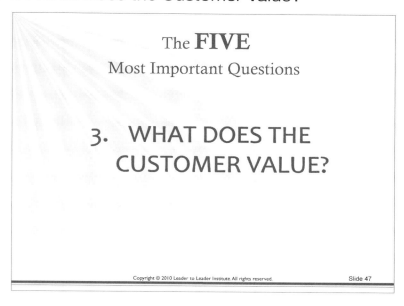

SAY   We are now going to take a look at Question 3: What Does the Customer Value? Drucker says this may be the most important question of all.

ASK   Why is it essential to understand what the customer values?

Note: Draw two to three responses and compare them with the following quote from Drucker and the points that follow it.

SHOW   Slide 48: Drucker on Customer Value[24]

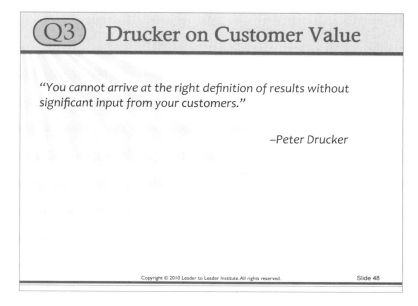

SAY   In self-assessment, what the customer values ties directly to how the organization defines, measures, and achieves results.

Remember that results are measured in changed lives.

SHOW   Slide 49: Value Defined

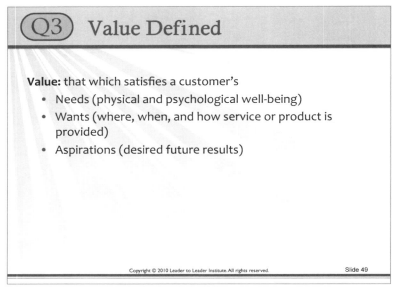

Note: Review definition and ask if there are any questions.

SAY   Note that what the customer values can be tangible or intangible.

Tangibles include housing for a homeless family or a higher grade-point average for a student involved in an after-school program.

Intangibles include a feeling of safety and peace of mind from having a permanent home . . . or an increased sense of curiosity and confidence to learn.

ASK   How do you know what the customer values?

Note: Ask for two to three responses and then state the following.

SAY   You need to ask the customer. To fully commit to Question 3, *you must listen to and learn from the customer*. Needs, wants, and aspirations can be complicated!

What the primary customer values is most important—serving the primary customer is the organization's reason for being.

But supporting customers also are important. The organization must pay attention to what supporting customers value in order to achieve results.

ASK What are some obstacles that prevent organizations from effectively engaging the customer in self-assessment?

Note: Ask participants to provide examples from their own experience. Ask for two to three responses and compare them with the points below. Examples are provided for each type of challenge.

SAY *Example 1:* Failing to challenge assumptions or "business-as-usual."

On page 40 of *The Five Most Important Questions You Will Ever Ask Your Organization*, Drucker describes a homeless shelter that was operating on the assumption that homeless customers valued nutritious meals and clean beds. When the staff talked with the customer, it discovered the customer valued most to regain stability in a safe shelter environment.

Example 2: Subordinating the mission for funding.

Organizations must never subordinate the mission for funding. Drucker discusses a museum being offered a donation of art from a donor on conditions that threatened the integrity of the organization. (See pages 15–16 of *The Five Most Important Questions You Will Ever Ask Your Organization*.)

ASK Why is it important to understand what the customer values? Who has an example?

Note: Ask for one or two examples and then review Kouzes on "value."

SHOW Slides 50 and 51: Kouzes on Value[25]

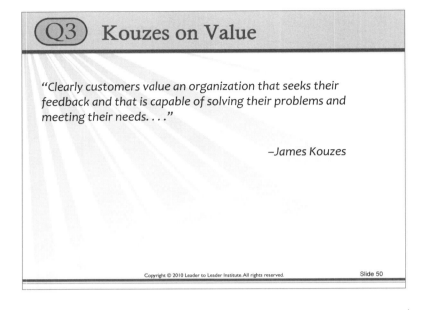

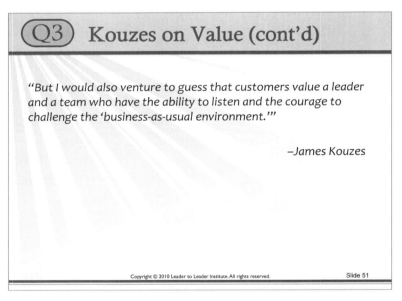

ASK Who here has used what the customer values to challenge "business-as-usual"?

Note: Ask for one or two examples. Ask participants how their organization's performance changed.

ASK How do you go about understanding what the customer values?

Note: Draw three to four responses and probe **how** to gather information on what the customer values. Compare the discussion with the following slide and points.

SHOW   Slide 52: Methods for Understanding What Customers Value

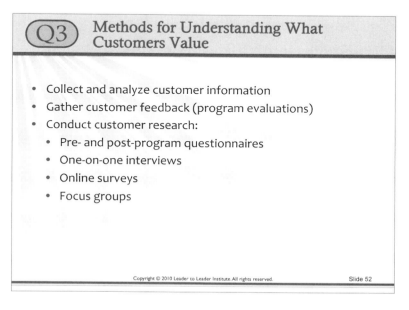

Q3 Methods for Understanding What Customers Value

- Collect and analyze customer information
- Gather customer feedback (program evaluations)
- Conduct customer research:
  - Pre- and post-program questionnaires
  - One-on-one interviews
  - Online surveys
  - Focus groups

Slide 52

SAY   Data gathering can be simple or complex. It can be as simple as using online survey tools, or it can involve more complex research techniques.

Also, when collecting customer information and feedback, it is important to think about customers who are not involved with your organization as well as those who have stopped being involved with your organization—find out why.

Exercise 5: Practical Application— What Does the Customer Value?

Purposes

- To explore what the customer values

- To discuss what knowledge the organization needs to gain from the customer

- To prepare the organization to explore "Value"

Time

Half-day training: 10 minutes

Full-day training: 30 minutes (5 for delivering instructions, 15 for small-group work, 10 for large-group discussion)

Two-day training: 60 minutes (5 to deliver instructions, 15 for groups to work on *primary customer*, 20 for groups to work on *supporting customers*, 20 for large-group discussion)

Worksheet(s)

Worksheets 3.1 and 3.2

Note: *Participants will work in the same groups they formed previously. (See the note on Practical Application exercises in Exercise 3.)*

Instructions

Half-day: In a half-day session, the goal will be to familiarize participants with the worksheets. As a full group, review Worksheets 3.1 and 3.2 and discuss any clarifying questions.

Full-day: Groups will use Worksheet 3.1, Question (a), and Worksheet 3.2—the first section on the primary customer. They will use Worksheet 3.1, Question (a), to discuss what the primary customer values. They should support their discussion with data. They will use Worksheet 3.2 to explore additional knowledge the organization needs to gather from the primary customer to understand what the customer values.

Two-day: Groups will follow the instructions above. Once they have discussed the primary customer, they can use the same worksheets to discuss the organization's *supporting customers*. (Worksheet 3.1, Question (b), and the sections of Worksheet 3.2 for supporting customers.)

You can introduce instructions for *supporting customer* once groups have finished exploring the primary customer.

Take the following steps to move through the exercise:

1. Remind participants to continue wearing two "hats"—one as a participant in dialogue, the other as facilitator. Ask them to take turns facilitating group dialogue. As they do they should focus on group "process"—how the group is communicating and making decisions.

2. If necessary, remind groups that the exercise will end in a large-group discussion, during which participants can explore how they will apply what they have learned during the exercise to their organization.

3. Deliver instructions for the exercise; make sure groups understand the exercise and how to use the worksheet(s).

4. Provide groups time warnings to ensure that they complete the exercise. Stop groups at the prescribed time and bring them back into a large-group discussion.

ASK   What does your primary customer value?

Note: Ask two or three groups to share what their primary customer values.

ASK   How did your groups decide what the primary customer values? Was there any discussion? Was there any need for further analysis?

Note: Ask for two or three responses and probe for more detail when appropriate.

ASK   What sources of data did you use to support your discussion?

Note: Ask for two or three responses and probe for more detail when appropriate.

ASK   What additional knowledge do you need in order to better understand what your primary customer values?

Note: Ask for two or three responses and probe for more detail when appropriate.

ASK (for two-day only) What do your supporting customers value?

Note: Ask from two or three groups to share what their supporting customers value.

ASK (for two-day only) How did your groups decide what the supporting customers value? Was there any discussion? Was there any need for further analysis?

Note: Ask for two or three responses and probe for more detail when appropriate.

ASK (for two-day only) What sources of data did you use to support your discussion?

Note: Ask for two or three responses and probe for more detail when appropriate.

ASK (for two-day only) What additional knowledge do you need to better understand what your supporting customers value?

Note: Ask for two or three responses and probe for more detail when appropriate.

ASK Now let's talk about process. What was it like to participate in dialogue on "Value"? What was it like to facilitate?

Note: Ask for two responses from the participants' point of view and two responses from the facilitators' point of view. If conducting a two-day session, instruct participants to think about both primary and supporting customers.

ASK What insights did you gain? What is needed for a productive dialogue on "Value"? What steps will you take to prepare your organization for a dialogue on "Value"?

*Note: Label a flip chart "Value." Work with the group to identify at least **five** steps and write them on the flip chart. Ask participants to set aside some pages in their notebooks to track design steps for "Value." To focus the group on process, you might ask*

- *Who in your organization will you ask to participate in a dialogue on "Value"?* (The board must be engaged in the dialogue; also supporting customers, such as staff and volunteers, who work closely with the primary customer. Research experts. The organization may also engage the primary customer directly in dialogue.)

- *What data will you gather and analyze to inform a dialogue on "Value"?* (customer research, and so on)

- *What qualities in a facilitator will you seek?*

- *How much time will you reserve for a dialogue on "Value"? What will the venue look like?*

- *What do you think will be the outcomes of the dialogue on "Value"?*

SHOW Slide 53: Practical Application

Practical Application

- *Participant Workbook* – Worksheets 3.1 - 3.3
- Environmental scan
- Customer research
- Internal data

Slide 53

SAY Remember there is an additional worksheet for Question 3 in the *Participant Workbook*. Worksheet 3.3 asks you to think about how you will gather additional knowledge you need from the customer.

When preparing your organization for self-assessment, it will be important for you to familiarize yourself with the worksheets, as well as the other resources listed here.

SHOW Slide 54: Question 3: Focus Points

> ## (Q3) Question 3: Focus Points
>
> - For Drucker, "What does the customer value?" may be the most important question an organization can ask.
> - Customer value is that which satisfies needs, wants, and aspirations.
> - The organization must be committed to listening to the customer.
>
>   Slide 54

ASK Here are the major points we have covered. Are there any questions before we conclude Question 3?

Note: If you're conducting the two-day session, this section is followed by a break and then Day One concludes with the first part of "Reflect on The Five Most Important Questions." You'll need to skip ahead to that section of this guide to complete Day One of the two-day session. You'll return to "What Are Our Results?" at the beginning of Day Two.

What Are Our Results?

Half-Day Training Time: 30 minutes

Time Breakdown (approximation)

- 10 minutes to present principles and terminology

- 20 minutes for Exercise 6: Practical Application—What Are Our Results?

Full-Day Training Time: 45 minutes

Time Breakdown (approximation)

- 20 minutes to present principles and terminology

- 25 minutes for Exercise 6: Practical Application—What Are Our Results?

Two-Day Training Time: 90 minutes

Time Breakdown (approximation)

- 30 minutes to present principles and terminology

- 60 minutes for Exercise 6: Practical Application—What Are Our Results?

Slides: 55–64

Focus Points

- *Results* are defined in changed lives—behavior, circumstances, health, hopes, competence, or capacity

- Results are always outside the organization

- The organization measures results (qualitatively and quantitatively) to appraise performance

- To achieve results, the organization

    - Concentrates its strengths

    - Abandons what it does not do well

    - Innovates

    - Analyzes

Related Worksheets in *Participant Workbook*

*Worksheet 4.1: How Do We Define Results?

Worksheet 4.2: How Do We Measure Results?

Worksheet 4.3: How Can We Improve Our Performance?

(*used as part of the small-group work at the end of the session)

Note: *For the half-day session, you can present the content, but likely will not have time for questions or discussion.*

SHOW Slide 55: What Are Our Results?

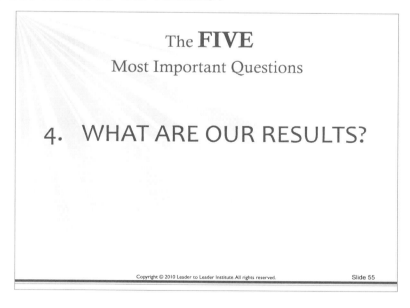

SAY Results are *humanized* in the Drucker process.

Through dialogue on results, an organization decides what difference it aims to make.

SHOW Slide 56: Drucker on Results[26]

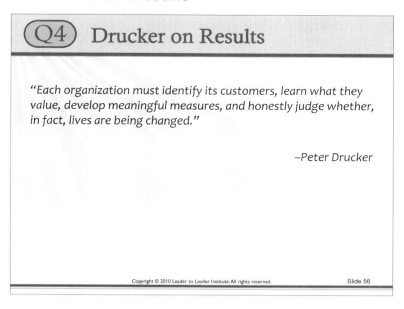

SAY Here is what Drucker says about results.

Note: *Review slide.*

ASK   Can anyone give an example of an organization that is outwardly focused on results?

Note: Draw one or two responses and probe how the organization(s) demonstrate an outward focus on changing lives.

SHOW   Slide 57: Results Defined

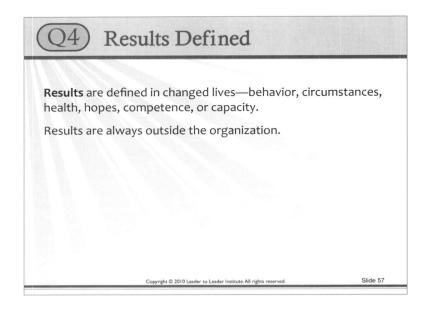

Note: Review definition of results.

ASK   How do you define results for your organization?

Note: Results need to be defined in terms of how the organization changes the life of the primary customer. If you need to, you can go back to the examples raised for organization(s) that are outwardly focused on results and ask participants how those organization(s) define results. Or, refer to pages 64 and 65 in the Participant Workbook, *which show the missions of three organizations, as well as how they define results.*

ASK   How do you measure results?

SHOW Slide 58: Measuring Results

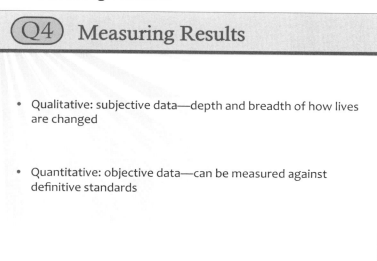

SAY Measures can be designed qualitatively or quantitatively, but they must relate with how the organization is making a difference in the life of the primary customer.

ASK Why use both types of measures?

Note: Draw one or two responses and compare with the following point.

SAY For Drucker, "These two types of measures are interwoven—they shed light on one another—and both are necessary to illuminate in what ways and to what extent lives are being changed."[27]

ASK Who can give an example of a qualitative measure?

*Note: Draw two to three responses. Make sure the measures are **qualitative**, not quantitative. For the purpose of this discussion, make sure measures demonstrate how the organization is making a difference in the life of the **primary customer**. If the measures offered do not, guide the group in thinking about better measures.*

Examples of qualitative measures include the primary customers of a homeless shelter self-reporting they have a greater sense of security and well-being when they find permanent housing, and the primary customers of an after-school program self-reporting an increased interest in learning and student achievement.

ASK   Who can give an example of a quantitative measure?

*Note: Draw two to three responses. Make sure the measures are **quantitative**, not qualitative. For the purpose of this discussion, make sure measures demonstrate how the organization is making a difference in the life of the **primary customer**. If the measures offered do not, guide the group in thinking about better measures.*

Examples of quantitative measures include the number of homeless families who regain permanent housing and the number of students who enroll in college.

SHOW   Slide 59: Achieving Results

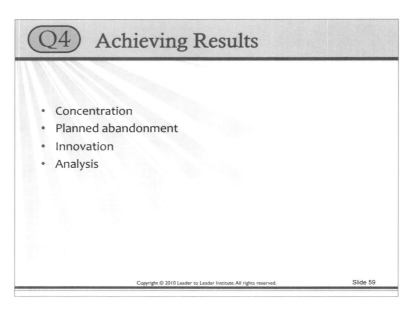

SAY   We've talked about how results are defined and measured. Now, let's talk about *how* to achieve results.

Self-assessment uses the terms *concentration*, *planned abandonment*, *innovation*, and *analysis* to guide this process.

These terms are introduced in your *Participant Workbook* during Question 4, but also are used during Question 5 when the organization revisits the mission, sets the goals, and develops the plan.

What do these terms mean?

Concentration is strengthening what works. The organization focuses on the programs and activities that contribute to achieving the right results.

The organization looks at the ways in which it can serve the customer exceptionally well—and how it can improve what it does exceptionally well.

Planned abandonment is removing programs and activities that are decreasing in relevance or not producing adequate results.

Drucker asks, "If we were not committed to this today, would we go into it? If the answer is no . . . how can we get out—fast?"*

Planned abandonment frees up resources and talent. To consider and follow-through with planned abandonment requires courage and discipline.

Innovation is change that creates a new dimension of performance. Innovation can take different forms: it can be a new program or service—or an enhanced process.

The organization uses further *analysis* to inform decision making and allocate resources.

ASK Are there any questions about concentration, planned abandonment, innovation, or analysis?

Note: *Field questions.*

*Stern, Gary. *The Drucker Foundation Self-Assessment Tool Process Guide*. San Francisco: Jossey-Bass, 1999, p. 54.

ASK Who here has an example [of concentration, planned abandonment, innovation, or analysis]?

SHOW Slide 60: A Delicate Balance

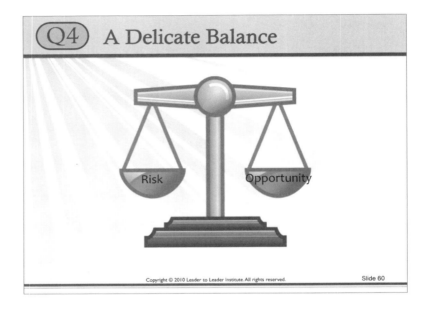

SAY Finally, it is important for the organization to weigh risk with opportunity as it thinks about how to improve performance and achieve results.

SHOW Slide 61: Rodin on Results[28]

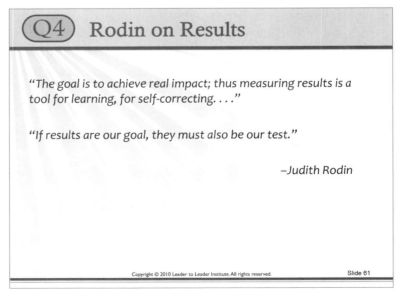

Note: *Review slide and move into practical application.*

Exercise 6: Practical Application—What Are Our Results?

Purposes

- To define and measure results

- To discuss how to achieve results

- To prepare the organization to explore "Results"

Time

Half-day training: 20 minutes

Full-day training: 25 minutes (3 for delivering instructions, 12 for small-group work, 10 for large-group discussion)

Two-day training: 60 minutes (5 to deliver instructions, 35 for small-group work, 20 for large-group discussion)

Worksheet(s)

Worksheets 4.1, 4.2, and 4.3

Note: *Participants will work in the same groups they formed previously. (See the note on Practical Application exercises in Exercise 3.)*

Instructions

Half-day: This can be conducted similarly to the full-day design. You'll need to shave a few minutes from both the small-group work and the large-group discussion.

Full-day: Groups will use Worksheets 4.1, 4.2, and 4.3, Question (a). They will use Worksheet 4.1 to define *one* result for the organization. They will use Worksheet 4.2 to design at least *one quantitative* measure and *one qualitative* measure. Groups should base their discussions on their work on "Mission," "Customer," and "Value."

For the purposes of this exercise, results should reflect how the organization changes the life of the primary customer.

Once groups have worked with results, they will use Worksheet 4.3, Question (a) to review the organization's programs and think of *two* ways to achieve results. This can include how to concentrate, or strengthen, abandon, innovate, and analyze.

Two-day: Groups will follow the instructions above, but they will

- Define two to three results
- Work with one result and decide how to measure it quantitatively and qualitatively—more than one of each type of measure can be developed
- Think of *five* ways to achieve results

Take the following steps to move through the exercise:

1. Remind participants to continue wearing two "hats"—one as a participant in dialogue, the other as facilitator. Ask them to take turns facilitating group dialogue. As they do they should focus on group "process"—how the group is communicating and making decisions.

2. If necessary, remind groups that the exercise will end in a large-group discussion, during which participants can explore how they will apply what they have learned to their organization.

3. Deliver instructions for the exercise; make sure groups understand the exercise and how to use the worksheet(s).

4. If groups have difficulty defining results, refer them to page 64 of the *Participant Workbook*, "How *Should* the Organization Define Results?"

5. Provide groups time warnings to ensure that they complete the exercise. Stop groups at the prescribed time and bring them back into a large-group discussion.

ASK How did you define your result(s)?

Note: *Ask two or three groups to share the result(s) they defined for the organization. For two-day workshops, engage more participants and go into more depth.*

ASK How did your group define your result(s)? Was there any discussion? Was there any need for further analysis?

> *Note: Ask for two or three responses and probe for more detail when appropriate. For two-day workshops, engage more participants and go into more depth.*

ASK How will you measure your result?

> *Note: Ask for responses from the same groups who shared their definition(s) for results. For two-day workshops, go into more depth.*

ASK What was it like to design measures?

> *Note: Ask for two or three responses. For two-day workshops, engage more participants and go into more depth.*

ASK How will you improve performance? How did you come to your decisions? Was there any discussion?

> *Note: Ask for two or three responses and probe for more detail when appropriate. For two-day workshops, engage more participants and go into more depth.*

ASK Now let's talk about process. What was it like to participate in dialogue on "Results"? What was it like to facilitate?

> *Note: Ask for two responses from the participants' point of view and two responses from the facilitator's point of view.*

ASK What insights did you gain? What is needed for a productive dialogue on "Results"? What steps will you take to prepare your organization for a dialogue on "Results"?

> *Note: Label a flip chart "Results." Work with the group to identify at least **five** steps and write them on the flip chart. Ask participants to set aside some pages in their notebooks to track design steps for "Results." To focus the group on process, you might ask*
>
> - *Who in your organization will you ask to participate in a dialogue on "Results"? (The board must be engaged in the dialogue; also staff members familiar with operations and organizational performance.)*
>
> - *What data will you gather and analyze to inform a dialogue on "Results"? (internal data)*

- *What qualities in a facilitator will you seek?*

- *How much time will you reserve for a dialogue on "Results"? What will the venue look like?*

- *What do you think will be the outcomes of the dialogue on "Results"?*

SHOW   Slide 62: Practical Application

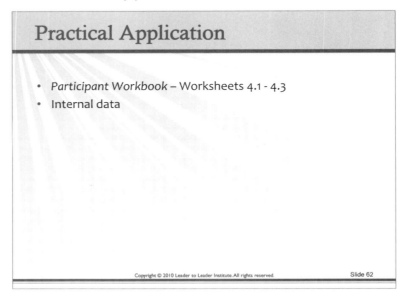

SAY   When preparing your organization for self-assessment, it will be important for you to familiarize yourself with the worksheets, as well as the other resources listed here.

SHOW   Slides 63 and 64: Question 4 Focus Points

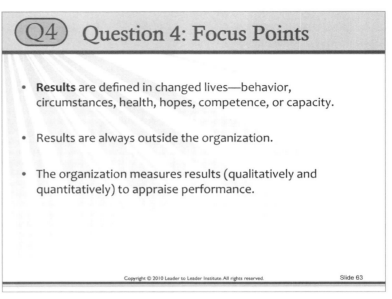

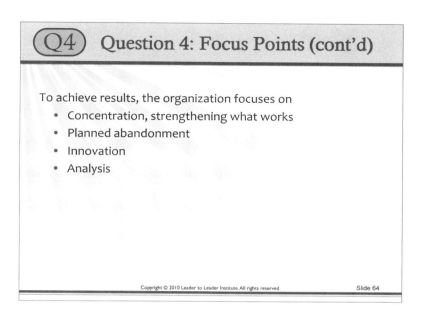

ASK These are the major points we have discussed. Are there any questions before we move onto Question 5?

What Is Our Plan?

Half-Day Training Time: 20 minutes

Time Breakdown (approximation)

- 10 minutes to present principles and terminology

- 10 minutes for Exercise 7: Practical Application—What Is Our Plan?

Full-Day Training Time: 40 minutes

Time Breakdown (approximation)

- 20 minutes to present principles and terminology

- 20 minutes for Exercise 7: Practical Application—What Is Our Plan?

Two-Day Training Time: 60 minutes

Time Breakdown (approximation)

- 30 minutes to present principles and terminology

- 30 minutes for Exercise 7: Practical Application—What Is Our Plan?

Slides: 65–74

Focus Points

- The plan is a concise summation of the organization's purpose and future direction

- The plan encompasses vision, mission, goals, objectives, action steps, a budget, and appraisal

- The board is responsible for revisiting the mission, determining goals, and approving the plan

- Management is responsible for developing objectives, action steps, and the budget

Related Worksheets in *Participant Workbook*

*Worksheet 5.1: What Is Our Mission?

 Worksheet 5.2: What Are Our Goals?

Worksheet 5.3: What Is Our Plan to Achieve Results for the Organization?

Worksheet 5.4: How Will We Communicate Our Mission, Plan, and Results?

(*used as part of the small-group work at the end of the session)

Note: *For the half-day session, you'll just have time to present the content. For the full-day session, you can allow limited time for questions and discussion.*

SHOW Slide 65: What Is Our Plan?

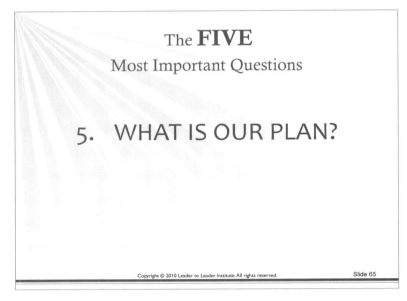

SHOW Slide 66: Drucker on Plan[29]

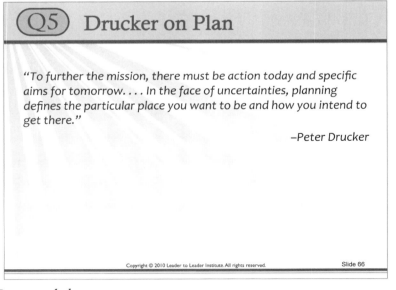

Note: Review slide.

SAY Throughout self-assessment, Drucker challenges us to look outside the window for trends that will have the greatest impact on our organizations. He asks us to listen to our customer and focus on results. But most of all, he challenges us to take action.

Self-assessment requires the organization's commitment to action—or it becomes only a planning exercise.

ASK How do we take what we have learned during self-assessment and convert it to action?

SHOW Slide 67: Plan Defined

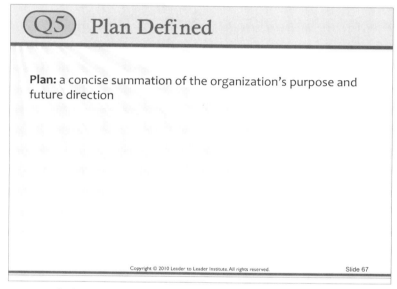

Note: Review definition of plan.

ASK Who can talk a little bit about what it is like to develop a plan? How do you go about it? What is your experience?

Note: Draw one or two accounts.

ASK What are the key components of the plan?

Note: Draw three to four responses from the group and compare with the following diagram and points.

SHOW Slide 68: Planning for Results

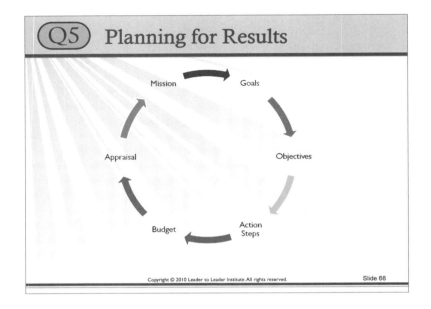

SAY Here is a diagram of the planning process. As you can see it is circular, not linear.

Note: Use the slide to move through each step of the planning process.

SAY Let's talk about how the plan is developed, as well as what the board is responsible for and what the management team is responsible for.

The board is responsible for developing the strategic part of the plan (the vision, mission, and goals), while the CEO, with input from the board and staff, is responsible for developing the tactical, or operational, part of the plan (the objectives, action steps, and budget that will allow the organization to further its mission and reach its goals).

The board develops and approves the **strategic** plan before the operational is developed and approved. The board chairman brings both parts of the plan before the board for action.

ASK What is the first step in developing the strategic plan?

Note: Take one or two responses.

SAY   The first step is to decide whether or not to revisit the *mission*. This is a board decision.

ASK   What is the second step?

Note: Take one or two responses.

SAY   The second step is to establish three to five *goals*. From the mission flow the organization's goals.

Goals are a set of aims that set the organization's fundamental, future direction.

They are few in number. Drucker says "if you have more than five goals, you have none."* The organization dilutes its efforts.

Goals guide the organization to concentrate resources for results, engage in planned abandonment, and innovate.

The organization may or may not develop a vision.

The vision is a picture of the organization's desired future. It is the board's responsibility to develop vision.

The vision of the desired future is painted first, before the organization establishes mission.

Example—Girl Scouts of Western Washington

Vision: *By building a diverse and connected community of girls and adults committed to lifelong stewardship and sustainability, Girl Scouts of Western Washington creates women leaders.*

Mission: *Building girls of Courage, Confidence, and Character who make the world a better place.*

ASK   What is the first step in developing the **operational** plan?

Note: Take one or two responses.

*Stern, Gary. *The Drucker Foundation Self-Assessment Tool Process Guide*. San Francisco: Jossey-Bass, 1999, p. 53.

SAY The first step is developing *objectives*.

Objectives are specific and measurable levels of achievement that move the organization toward its goals.

Management is responsible for developing the objectives, which are approved by the board.

Next, management develops *action steps* and the *budget*.

Action steps are detailed plans and activities that meet an organization's objectives.

They show how resources will be used and who will do it, as well as the timeframe for completion.

Action steps are developed with input from the people who will carry them out.

ASK Who has engaged staff in developing action steps? How did this affect your organization's ability to carry out the plan?

SAY Drucker says, "Everyone with a role should have the opportunity to give input. This looks incredibly slow. But when the plan is completed, the next day everyone understands it."*

The *budget* is the commitment of resources necessary to implement the plan.

Management is responsible for developing the action steps and budget, which are approved by the board.

Finally, *appraisal* is the process for monitoring and meeting objectives and achieving results. It is the point at which action steps for meeting objectives may be modified on the basis of experience or changed conditions. The plan is a living document to be used to achieve results. The board and the management team are involved in ongoing appraisal.

ASK Are there any questions about the planning process?

*Stern, Gary. *The Drucker Foundation Self-Assessment Tool Process Guide*. San Francisco: Jossey-Bass, 1999, p. 55.

Note: *Field any questions. If participants would like to see an example of a plan, you can use the "Sample Plan" slides for the Girl Scouts of Western Washington (slides 69–72). Otherwise, skip ahead to Slide 73.*

SHOW   Slide 69 (optional): Sample Plan 1

SHOW   Slide 70 (optional): Sample Plan 2

SHOW Slide 71 (optional): Sample Plan 3

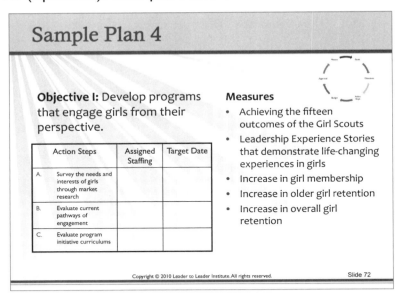

SHOW Slide 72 (optional): Sample Plan 4

SHOW   Slide 73: Rangan on Plan[30]

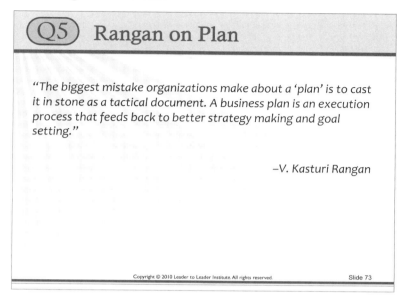

ASK   What do you think about Rangan's statement?

Note: Review "Rangan on Plan" and draw two to three comments.

ASK   Once an organization has approved the plan, it is time to implement it. What are some ways the organization can ensure the plan is implemented successfully?

Note: Ask for three to four responses and compare them with the following steps to implement the plan:

- *The leaders (board chairman, board, and the chief executive officer) communicate the plan to the organization and its customers.*

- *Leadership prepares the organization for strategic and organizational change (concentration, innovation, planned abandonment, and so on).*

- *Appraise performance and make course corrections.*

Exercise 7: Practical Application— What Is Our Plan?

Purpose

- To prepare the organization to develop and implement the "Plan"

Time

Half-day training: 10 minutes

Full-day training: 20 minutes (3 for delivering instructions, 12 for small-group work, 5 for large-group discussion)

Two-day training: 30 minutes (3 to deliver instructions, 17 for small-group work, 10 for large-group discussion)

Worksheet(s)

Worksheets 5.1, 5.2, 5.3, and 5.4

Note: *Participants will work in the same groups they formed previously. (See the note on Practical Application exercises, see Exercise 3.)*

Instructions

Half-day: As a whole group, quickly look over Worksheets 5.1, 5.2, 5.3, and 5.4. Answer any clarifying questions.

Full-day: Groups will use Worksheet 5.1. For Question (b), groups will decide if the mission needs to be revisited. If yes, they will use Question (c) to develop a new mission statement. Groups will use Worksheet 5.2 to decide on one to two goals for the organization.

Two-day: Same instructions as above, but have groups consider Question (a) on Worksheet 5.1. The groups can work through as many goals as time allows for Worksheet 5.2. They also may use Worksheet 5.3 to work on objectives for one of the goals.

Take the following steps to move through the exercise:

1. Remind participants to continue wearing two "hats"—one as a participant in dialogue, the other as facilitator. Ask them to take turns facilitating group dialogue. As they do they should focus on group "process"—how the group is communicating and making decisions.

2. If necessary, remind groups that the exercise will end in a large-group discussion, during which participants can explore how they will apply what they have learned to their organization.

3. Deliver instructions for the exercise; make sure groups understand the exercise and how to use the worksheet(s).

4. Provide groups time warnings to ensure that they complete the exercise. Stop groups at the prescribed time and bring them back into a large-group discussion.

ASK How many groups decided to revisit mission?

Note: Take a quick count. If some groups revisited mission, ask them why they decided to do so. Ask them to offer what they recommend for a new mission. Probe the groups on how they developed the new mission—what the major decisions were and so on. If some groups decided not to revisit mission, ask one or two of them why.

ASK What are your goals?

Note: Ask two or three groups to list their goals.

ASK How did your group decide on your goals? Was there any discussion? Was there any need for further analysis?

Note: Ask for two or three responses and probe for more detail when appropriate. For two-day workshops, ask more participants and go into more depth.

ASK Now let's talk about process. What was it like to participate in dialogue on "Plan"? What was it like to facilitate?

Note: Ask for two responses from the participants' point of view and two responses from the facilitator's point of view.

ASK What insights did you gain? What is needed for a productive dialogue on "Plan"? What steps will you take to prepare your organization for a dialogue on "Plan"?

*Note: Label a flip chart "Plan." Work with the group to identify at least **five** steps and write them on the flip chart. Ask participants to set aside some pages in their notebooks to track design steps for "Plan." To focus the group on process, you might ask*

- *Who in your organization will you ask to participate in a dialogue on "Results"?* (The board must be engaged in developing the strategic plan; staff members familiar with operations may provide input to the operational plan.)

- *What data will you gather and analyze to inform a dialogue on "Plan"?* (internal data)

- *What qualities in a facilitator will you seek?*

- *How much time will you reserve for a dialogue on "Plan"? What will the venue look like?* (The plan will be developed in two stages. First, the board will use the outcomes of facilitated dialogue to develop and approve the strategic plan [vision, mission, and goals]. Then the chief executive officer will develop the operational plan for board approval [objectives, action steps, and budget].)

- *What do you think will be the outcomes of the dialogue on "Plan"?*

SHOW   Slide 74: Question 5: Focus Points

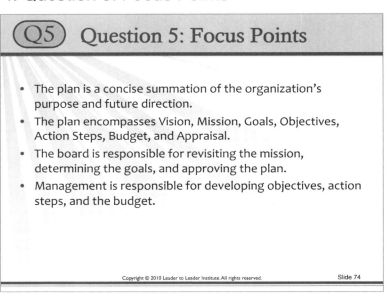

ASK   These are the major points we have discussed. Are there any questions?

Reflect on The Five Most Important Questions

- Half-day training time: 10 minutes
- Full-day training time: 30 minutes
- Two-day training time: Day 1, 40 minutes; Day 2, 60 minutes
- Slide: 75

Exercise 8: Reflect on The Five Most Important Questions

Purpose

- To think about how self-assessment has had an impact on participants' understanding of and approach to strategic planning.

Time

Half-day training: 10 minutes

Full-day training: 30 minutes (5 for delivering instructions, 15 for small-group work, 10 for group debriefs)

Two-day training: Day 1: 40 minutes (5 to deliver instructions, 20 for small-group work, 15 for large-group discussion)

Day 2: 60 minutes (5 to deliver instructions, 35 for small-group work, 20 for large-group discussion)

Note: *For the half-day session, you'll just review the questions on slide 75 as a group and have a brief discussion.*

For the two-day workshop, you will hold a session on both days to reflect on the self-assessment framework. For Day 1, mention that participants will reflect on the first three questions. For Day 2, they will reflect on all five questions.

Instructions

1. Use this exercise to get participants out of their chairs and walking around. Designate a reporter from each group to share findings during the full-group discussion at the end of the exercise.

2. Ask participants

   - What did you hear during the workshop?

   - What does it mean?

   The groups should spend the first part of the exercise sharing their reflections and thoughts—using flip charts or whiteboards to record major points. If flip charts or whiteboards are not available, have groups use a notepad to record their thoughts.

3. *Optional: use slide 75 and ask groups to use the questions on the slide to guide their discussion.*

SHOW Slide 75 (optional): Reflect on The Five Most Important Questions

The Five Most Important Questions

Reflecting on The Five Most Important Questions:
1. Has self-assessment had an impact on my approach to strategic planning? How?
2. What has left the greatest impression? Reflect on
   - Drucker's principles and language
   - The *Tool*: The Five Most Important Questions, the *Participant Workbook*, facilitated dialogue, and so on
3. What will I do differently?

Copyright © 2010 Leader to Leader Institute. All rights reserved.   Slide 75

4. After the allotted time, bring participants back into a discussion with the full group. Ask each group to report on what was discussed. Probe the groups for more detail. Note any emerging themes and clarify any confusion about self-assessment if it emerges.

Bring Self-Assessment to Your Organization

- Half-day training time: 30 minutes

- Full-day training time: 60 minutes

- Two-day training time: 90 minutes

Exercise 9: Self-Assessment—Process Design

Purpose

- For participants to learn how to design a self-assessment process that meets the planning needs of their organizations

Time

Half-day training: 30 minutes (10 for content presentation, 10 for small-group work, 10 for large-group discussion)

Full-day training: 60 minutes (10 for delivering instructions, 35 for small-group work, 15 for group debriefs)

Two-day training: 90 minutes (10 to deliver instructions, 45 for small-group work, 35 for large-group discussion)

Slides: 76 and 77

Materials

Process steps from Practical Application exercises (at least five steps for each question)

Preparation

1. Read Section 1 in the *Facilitator's Guide* and be prepared to explain the major components of self-assessment (gain commitment, design, conduct, and take action). You also may refer back to the "Overview of Self-Assessment" in this script to reinforce major points.

2. Display around the room the process steps that you recorded during the Practical Application exercises. If you have not used a flip chart or whiteboard to record these steps, you can photocopy written notes for participants or read them out loud and have participants write them down. Ask participants to refer to the notes they took during the Practical Application exercises.

SHOW Slides 76 and 77 (optional): Organizational Self-Assessment

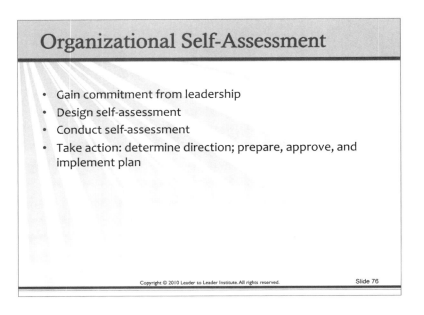

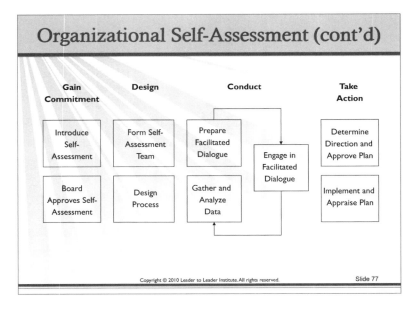

Instructions

1. Break participants into groups of two or three. Participants may work alone if they prefer. Participants from the same organization should be grouped together.

2. Review the major points of designing self-assessment and field any questions participants have about process design.

   First, ask participants to review their notes and the process steps on display. If space permits, encourage people to walk around and view the steps. When participants are ready, they will work with their groups to create a basic self-assessment design for their organizations.

   Groups will use the process steps on display to think through organizational requirements for self-assessment. Ask participants to think about

   - Time and resource needs

   - Who will be a part of the Self-Assessment Team

   - Facilitator requirements

   - Data gathering and analysis

   - Dialogue design—length, frequency, and so on

3. Ask participants to think through how self-assessment can be aligned to the governance activity of their organizations.

   Groups will prepare a working draft of their design that includes the following:

   - The organization's purpose and expected outcomes for conducting self-assessment

   - A detailed plan for each step for self-assessment (gain commitment, design, conduct, and take action)

   - A time and resource estimate

4. As groups work on their designs, they should note any questions they might have for their board, management team, or the facilitator that will inform the design. For instance,

- What outcomes will the board expect to see from self-assessment?

- Who will manage the self-assessment process?

5. During the exercise, observe group work and field questions.

6. After the allotted time, ask groups to report on their progress and what they are discovering with the process designs. Ask two to three groups to share their design. You can lead a discussion and help groups refine their designs, as well as work through any questions about design. Make sure groups from different organizations have a chance to share.

Note: For the half-day session, you'll present the content on organizational self-assessment (Step 2 above). In small groups, participants can then begin to work on Step 3. You then can bring the whole group back together to discuss ideas and respond to questions.

Closing and Evaluation

SHOW   Slide 78: "What do you want to be remembered for?"

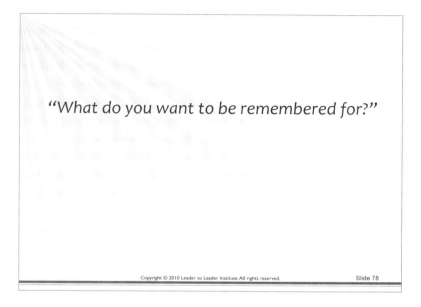

"What do you want to be remembered for?"

SAY   What do you want to be remembered for?

Note: Thank the group for its energy, effort, and inquisitiveness. Refer back to the purpose and goals of the workshop.

ASK   Did we achieve our goals today? Do you feel you have a good understanding of Peter Drucker's principles and terminology?

Note: Probe for responses.

ASK   Do you feel you have gained sufficient experience working with the *Self-Assessment Tool*?

Note: Probe for responses.

ASK   Who here feels they will bring self-assessment to their organization?

Note: Probe for responses. Ask participants to complete an evaluation of the workshop and field any last comments and questions.

Appendix
Sample Documents

The following documents can be found in this Appendix:

- Sample agenda for "What Is Our Mission?"

- Sample facilitated dialogue summary

- Sample depth interview

- Sample customer research designs

Sample Agenda for "What Is Our Mission?"

Objectives

1. Assess the mission and determine if it needs to be revisited.

2. Identify the trends that will have the greatest impact on the organization.

3. Discuss the most promising opportunities.

Agenda

1. Welcome, introductions, overview, and ground rules.

2. Initiate discussion on the mission (using Worksheet 1.1), and determine if the mission needs to be revisited (using Worksheet 1.2).

3. Identify the trends that will have the greatest impact on the organization (using Worksheet 1.3).

4. Take a break.

5. Explore the organization's opportunities and determine the most promising ones (using Worksheet 1.4).

Sample Facilitated Dialogue Summary[31]

Two self-assessment sessions were held with board and staff to discuss mission, the customer, and value. Fourteen board members and all staff were present. The group explored Questions 1, 2, and 3 using the *Participant Workbook*. The meeting was tape recorded, and the following summary reflects input from flip-chart notes, participant notes, and recorded comments.

Does the mission need to be revisited?

The general consensus was that the mission needs to be revisited. The following comments were made:

- Too restrictive on who we serve

- Too long

- Need clearer statement

- New mission should define our purpose

What are the most significant opportunities?

- Potential to influence and play a significant role in area school-to-work curricula development and service design

- Potential for new funds from local sources

- Potential to influence and play a significant role in area welfare-to-work philosophies, service design, and funding patterns

- Potential to have a broader impact on ability of service area residents to find and keep employment and advance to better-paying jobs

- Ability to influence state and county employment service policies and funding decisions (already on "right" committees, attending forums, visiting elected officials)

- Potential to provide greater value to area employers by helping to fill positions, train, and provide ongoing human resources support

Who is the primary customer?

Participants used the following groups to define the primary customer:

- Dislocated workers
- Welfare recipients/AFDC recipients
- Disadvantaged youth and adults
- Older workers
- Underemployed
- Low-income, single heads of households
- Non-English-speaking
- At-risk youth
- People in crisis
- Unemployed
- Employers

Participants agreed on the following definition of primary customers:

- People who are unemployed, underemployed, or at risk for unemployment

Participants agreed employers are *supporting* customers and are extremely important in the organization's ability to achieve results.

How will the primary customer change?

More customers will be

- Welfare recipients
- Non-English-speaking
- Dislocated workers
- Single parents

- Older workers

- People with disabilities

- Low-skilled

- Involved in gangs

More customers will have

- Multiple barriers to employment

- Family dysfunction, susceptibility to violence

- Legal problems

- Chemical dependency

- Mental illness

What knowledge do we want to gain from our primary customer?

- What are our primary customers' employment aspirations?

- What do customers feel they need to change in their lives to realize aspirations?

- What are the barriers to employment, according to the customer?

- What skills do primary customers want to develop?

- What employment-related services are desired?

- What hours and locations are convenient?

- How quickly would primary customers like service to be available once they contact us?

- How satisfied have our primary customers been with our service? What do they value most?

Sample Depth Interview[32]

Here is a set of basic depth-interview questions. If pointed issues have already arisen through the self-assessment process, additional questions may be added.

- What is your role with [the organization] and what is the length of your involvement?

- The current mission of the organization is [add mission here]. Do you believe the mission should be revisited? Why or why not?

- What do you see are the trends that will have the greatest impact on the organization in the coming years?

- What are the most significant opportunities?

- Who is the organization's primary customer? What does the primary customer value?

- How should the organization determine results?

- What should be the organization's results?

- What programs should be strengthened, considered for abandonment, or analyzed?

- Are there internal systems that should be assessed for potential improvement?

- Are there innovations the organization should consider?

- If it were up to you to set the organization's overarching goals for the future, what would they be?

- Is there any other aspect of self-assessment you would like to comment on?

Sample Customer Research Designs[33]

Large-scale customer research projects can reach hundreds of customers, while others contact a handful. Here are five design examples:

1. A national membership organization took six months to

   - Hire a research firm to conduct five hundred telephone interviews and produce a detailed analysis.
   - Use a paid professional to design and analyze responses from a questionnaire that one hundred local presidents used to interview each other during a national meeting.
   - Use a paid professional to train self-assessment participants as focus group facilitators and recorders who, in turn, ran fourteen focus groups simultaneously during a national conference. The professional then summarized findings.
   - Use a paid professional to train a Self-Assessment Team member who, in turn, prepared other self-assessment participants to conduct twenty face-to-face interviews with supporting customers, with results analyzed by the Steering Team member.

2. An art museum contracted with a market research firm and took three months to

   - Hold a video-taped series of focus groups with two proposed new customer groups that historically had not visited the museum in great numbers.
   - Edit highlights of the videotapes into a fifteen-minute segment as part of a special presentation of findings for self-assessment participants and later the board.

3. A local public health organization took six weeks to

   - Use staff to conduct and analyze a mail-back customer satisfaction survey.

4. A large United Way branch took five months to

   - Use a paid consultant to coach a staff member in developing interview and focus group formats using a blend of original questions and a standard United Way of America format.
   - Use volunteer research professionals and student interns under the direction of a pro bono research firm to analyze responses from a survey generated by the Self-Assessment Team of two hundred leadership donors and volunteers.

- Develop an interview format with the assistance of a school superintendent, train United Way board members, and complete interviews with elementary school principals in board members' home school districts.

5. A county government assessing services for homeless people formed a partnership with a research foundation that helped the county to

- Design a face-to-face interview format.
- Recruit and train one hundred volunteers, including self-assessment participants, to conduct three hundred interviews with homeless people in shelters across the county in one night.
- Analyze results and produce a summary report.

Recommended Resources

Other Works by Peter Drucker

Drucker, Peter F. *The Effective Executive: The Definitive Guide to Getting the Right Things Done*. Oxford: Butterworth-Heinemann, 2007.

Drucker, Peter F. *Innovation and Entrepreneurship*. New York: Harper Paperbacks, 2006.

Drucker, Peter F. *Management: Tasks, Responsibilities, Practices—Revised Edition*. New York: HarperCollins, 2008.

Drucker, Peter F. *Managing the Non-Profit Organization*. New York: Harper Paperbacks, 2006.

Leadership and Management Resources

Ackoff, Russell L., and Addison, Herbert J. *Systems Thinking for Curious Managers: With 40 New Management f-Laws*. Devon, UK: Triarchy Press, 2010.

Block, Peter. *Community: The Structure of Belonging*. San Francisco: Berrett-Koehler, 2009.

Bonk, Kathy, Griggs, Henry, and Tynes, Emily. *The Jossey-Bass Guide to Strategic Communications for Nonprofits*. San Francisco: Jossey-Bass, 1999.

Burton, Richard M., DeSanctis, Gerardine, and Obel, Børge. *Organizational Design: A Step-by-Step Approach*. Cambridge: Cambridge University Press, 2006.

Carter, Louis, Goldsmith, Marshall, and Ulrich, David. *Best Practices in Leadership Development and Organization Change: How the Best Companies Ensure Meaningful Change and Sustainable Leadership*. San Francisco: Pfeiffer, 2004.

Carttar, Paul, Colby, Susan, and Stone, Nan. "Zeroing in on Impact." *Stanford Social Innovation Review*, Fall 2004.

Collins, Jim. *Good to Great and the Social Sectors*. Boulder: Jim Collins, 2005.

Dalton, James G. *From Scan to Plan: Managing Change in Associations*. Washington, DC: American Society of Association Executives Foundation, 2004.

Gross, T. Scott. *Positively Outrageous Service: How to Delight and Astound Your Customers and Win Them for Life*. Chicago: Dearborn Trade Publishing, 2004.

Logan, Dave, and Zaffron, Steve. *The Three Laws of Performance: Rewriting the Future of Your Organization and Your Life*. San Francisco: Jossey-Bass, 2009.

Morrisey, George L. *Morrisey on Planning, A Guide to Strategic Thinking: Building Your Planning Foundation*. San Francisco: Jossey-Bass, 1996.

Osborne, David, and Popovich, Mark G. *Creating High-Performance Government Organizations*. San Francisco: Jossey-Bass, 1998.

Facilitation Resources

Cooperrider, David L., and Whitney, Diana. *Appreciative Inquiry: A Positive Revolution in Change*. San Francisco: Berrett-Koehler, 2005.

Goleman, Daniel. *Working with Emotional Intelligence*. New York: Bantam-Dell, 2006.

Scharmer, C. Otto. *Theory U: Leading from the Future as it Emerges, The Social Technology of Presencing*. San Francisco: Berrett-Koehler, 2009.

Stanfield, R. Brian. *The Art of Focused Conversation: 100 Ways to Access Group Wisdom in the Workplace*. Gabriola Island, British Columbia: New Society Publishers, 2000.

Wilkinson, Michael. *The Secrets of Facilitation: The S.M.A.R.T. Guide to Getting Results with Groups*. San Francisco: Jossey-Bass, 2004.

Notes

1. The Peter F. Drucker Foundation for Nonprofit Management, *The Drucker Foundation Self-Assessment Tool Participant Workbook* (San Francisco: Jossey-Bass, 1999), p. 7.

2. Gary Stern, *The Drucker Foundation Self-Assessment Tool Process Guide* (San Francisco: Jossey-Bass, 1999), pp. 3–5.

3. Stern, *Self-Assessment Tool Process Guide,* pp. 9–10.

4. Peter F. Drucker Foundation, *Self-Assessment Tool Participant Workbook,* p. 56.

5. Constance Rossum, *The Peter F. Drucker Foundation for Nonprofit Management: How to Assess Your Nonprofit Organization with Peter Drucker's Five Most Important Questions User Guide* (San Francisco: Jossey-Bass, 1993), p. 13.

6. Stern, *Self-Assessment Tool Process Guide,* pp. 31–32.

7. Peter F. Drucker Foundation, *Self-Assessment Tool Participant Workbook,* p. 35.

8. Peter F. Drucker Foundation, *Self-Assessment Tool Participant Workbook,* p. 10.

9. Stern, *Self-Assessment Tool Process Guide,* pp. 83–84.

10. ASAE, *From Scan to Plan: Integrating Trends into the Strategy-Making Process—Executive Summary* (Washington, DC: Foundation of the American Society of Association Executives, 2003), p. 4.

11. Stern, *Self-Assessment Tool Process Guide,* pp. 35–36.

12. Stern, *Self-Assessment Tool Process Guide,* pp. 67–70.

13. Rossum, *How to Assess Your Nonprofit Organization,* p. 15.

14. The Peter F. Drucker Foundation for Nonprofit Management, *Lessons in Leadership Facilitator's Guide* (San Francisco: Jossey-Bass, 1998), p. 4.

15. Leader to Leader Institute, *Courage to Lead Facilitator's Script*, internal company document, p. 3.

16. Stern, *Self-Assessment Tool Process Guide*, p. 23.

17. Peter F. Drucker, *Managing the Nonprofit Organization: Principles and Practices* (New York: HarperCollins, 1990), p. 124.

18. Leader to Leader Institute, *The Five Most Important Questions You Will Ever Ask About Your Organization* (San Francisco: Jossey-Bass, 2008), p. 14.

19. Leader to Leader Institute, *Five Most Important Questions*, p. 17.

20. ASAE, *From Scan to Plan*, p. 4.

21. Leader to Leader Institute, *Five Most Important Questions*, p. 25.

22. Leader to Leader Institute, *Five Most Important Questions*, p. 32.

23. Leader to Leader Institute, *Five Most Important Questions*, p. 28.

24. Stern, *Self-Assessment Tool Process Guide*, p. 4.

25. Leader to Leader Institute, *Five Most Important Questions*, p. 46.

26. Leader to Leader Institute, *Five Most Important Questions*, p. 52.

27. Leader to Leader Institute, *Five Most Important Questions*, pp. 52–53.

28. Leader to Leader Institute, *Five Most Important Questions*, pp. 58–59.

29. Leader to Leader Institute, *Five Most Important Questions*, pp. 65–66.

30. Leader to Leader Institute, *Five Most Important Questions*, p. 73.

31. Stern, *Self-Assessment Tool Process Guide*, pp. 62–67.

32. Stern, *Self-Assessment Tool Process Guide*, pp. 85–89.

33. Stern, *Self-Assessment Tool Process Guide*, pp. 71–73.

Note: Additional references located on pages 62, 99, 111, and 112 of this publication.

Acknowledgments

We are deeply grateful to the leaders, facilitators, and organizations that have contributed their time, inquisitiveness, and expertise to the third edition of *The Five Most Important Questions Self-Assessment Tool*. Over one hundred leaders representing more than seventy organizations helped field test the *Tool*.

We thank the leaders and facilitators who have worked tirelessly to bring Peter Drucker's *Self-Assessment Tool* to the social sector. We would like to thank Constance Rossum for her assistance in developing the first edition and Gary Stern for assisting in developing the second edition. Among the many individuals who helped shape the third edition are Derek Bell, Theresa Berenato, Dee Ann Boyd, Risa Cohn, Cathy Crosky, Susan Diamond, Carla Grantham, Justine Green, Lawrence Greenspan, Kathy Long Holland, Lee Igel, Irv Katz, Patricia Lewis, Matthew MacPherson, Michael Millar, Maria Carpenter Ort, Peggy Morrison Outon, Katherina Rosqueta, Doug Schallau, Kevin S. Smith, Iain Somerville, Bonita and Mark Thompson, Robert Clifford Uerz, and Tamara Woodbury.

Special thanks go to Frances Hesselbein for her guidance and her commitment to the social sector and performance excellence; she has been a tireless champion for Peter Drucker's work and for bringing The Five Most Important Questions to the social sector. Our appreciation goes to Jesse Wiley, our editorial partner at Jossey-Bass/Wiley, as well as to Susan Rachmeler and Nina Kreiden, who helped develop and produce the publications there. We thank Cathey Brown and Claire Walden for their work developing, editing and field testing this revised edition.

We would like to thank the Bright China Social Fund and the Buford Foundation for their generosity in making this edition of the *Tool* possible. We also thank the American Management Association and the Women Presidents' Organization for supporting The Five Most Important Questions workshops.

Our final thanks go to Peter F. Drucker for his dedication to the effective organization, for his contributions to management literature and practices, and for his support and contributions to the social sector. Without him, his wisdom and his passion, the Leader to Leader Institute would not exist and publishing these materials would not be possible.

THE Five
MOST IMPORTANT
QUESTIONS
Self-Assessment Tool

3RD EDITION

PARTICIPANT WORKBOOK

PETER F. DRUCKER

Leader
to Leader
INSTITUTE

JOSSEY-BASS
A Wiley Imprint
www.josseybass.com

About the Leader to Leader Institute

Established in 1990 as the Peter F. Drucker Foundation for Nonprofit Management, the Leader to Leader Institute furthers its mission—to strengthen the leadership of the social sector—by providing social sector leaders with essential leadership wisdom, inspiration, and resources to lead for innovation and to build vibrant social sector organizations. It is this essential social sector, in collaboration with its partners in the private and public sectors, that changes lives and builds a society of healthy children, strong families, decent housing, safe neighborhoods, good schools, and work that dignifies, all embraced by the diverse, inclusive, cohesive community that cares about all of its people.

The Leader to Leader Institute strengthens the leadership of the social sector by providing resources and support for

- Managing for the mission

- Making innovation part of strategy

- Developing productive partnerships, collaborations, and alliances

- Facilitating self-assessment

- Promoting and building richly diverse, inclusive organizations and communities

Leader to Leader Institute
320 Park Avenue, 3rd Floor
New York, NY 10022-6839
Telephone: (212) 224-1174
Fax: (212) 224-2508
E-mail: contact@leadertoleader.org, Website: www.leadertoleader.org

Other Publications from the Leader to Leader Institute

The Organization of the Future 2: Visions, Strategies, and Insights on Managing in a New Era, *Frances Hesselbein, Marshall Goldsmith, Editors*

The Five Most Important Questions You Will Ever Ask About Your Organization, *Peter F. Drucker with contributions from Jim Collins, Philip Kotler, Jim Kouzes, Judith Rodin, V. Kasturi Rangan, and Frances Hesselbein*

Leader to Leader 2: Enduring Insights on Leadership from the Leader to Leader Institute's Award-Winning Journal, *Frances Hesselbein, Alan Shrader, Editors*

In Extremis Leadership, *Thomas A. Kolditz*

The Leader of the Future 2, *Frances Hesselbein, Marshall Goldsmith, Editors*

Leadership Lessons from West Point, *Major Doug Crandall, Editor*

Leading Organizational Learning: Harnessing the Power of Knowledge, *Marshall Goldsmith, Howard Morgan, Alexander J. Ogg*

Be*Know*Do: Leadership the Army Way, *Frances Hesselbein, General Eric K. Shinseki, Editors*

Hesselbein on Leadership, *Frances Hesselbein*

Peter F. Drucker: An Intellectual Journey (video), *Leader to Leader Institute*

The Collaboration Challenge, *James E. Austin*

Meeting the Collaboration Challenge Workbook, *The Drucker Foundation*

On Leading Change: A Leader to Leader Guide, *Frances Hesselbein, Rob Johnston, Editors*

On High-Performance Organizations: A Leader to Leader Guide, *Frances Hesselbein, Rob Johnston, Editors*

On Creativity, Innovation, and Renewal: A Leader to Leader Guide, *Frances Hesselbein, Rob Johnston, Editors*

On Mission and Leadership: A Leader to Leader Guide, *Frances Hesselbein, Rob Johnston, Editors*

Leading for Innovation, *Frances Hesselbein, Marshall Goldsmith, Iain Somerville, Editors*

Leading in a Time of Change (video), *Peter F. Drucker, Peter M. Senge, Frances Hesselbein*

Leading in a Time of Change Viewer's Workbook, *Peter F. Drucker, Peter M. Senge, Frances Hesselbein*

Leading Beyond the Walls, *Frances Hesselbein, Marshall Goldsmith, Iain Somerville, Editors*

The Organization of the Future, *Frances Hesselbein, Marshall Goldsmith, Richard Beckhard, Editors*

The Community of the Future, *Frances Hesselbein, Marshall Goldsmith, Richard Beckhard, Richard F. Schubert, Editors*

Leader to Leader: Enduring Insights on Leadership from the Drucker Foundation, *Frances Hesselbein, Paul Cohen, Editors*

Excellence in Nonprofit Leadership (video), *Featuring Peter F. Drucker, Max De Pree, Frances Hesselbein, Michele Hunt; Moderated by Richard F. Schubert*

Excellence in Nonprofit Leadership Workbook and Facilitator's Guide, *Peter F. Drucker Foundation for Nonprofit Management*

Lessons in Leadership (video), *Peter F. Drucker*

Lessons in Leadership Workbook and Facilitator's Guide, *Peter F. Drucker*

The Leader of the Future, *Frances Hesselbein, Marshall Goldsmith, Richard Beckhard, Editors*

Contents

Foreword

"You say we should achieve excellence, but how do we know when we get there?" was the most compelling question the Peter Drucker Foundation, now the Leader to Leader Institute, heard in the fall of 1990, when our work began. This *Self-Assessment Tool,* in its third edition, is our continued response.

Remarkable opportunities exist for those who would lead their enterprises and this country into a new kind of society—of healthy children, strong families, good schools, decent housing, and work that dignifies, all embraced by a cohesive, inclusive community that cares about all its people. In this period of unprecedented worldwide societal transformation, leaders from all sectors will dare to see life and community whole. They will strive to address the needs of body, mind, and spirit. They will view their work as an amazing opportunity to express everything within that gives passion and light to living. They will have the courage to lead from the front on issues, principles, vision, and mission that becomes the star to steer by.

Self-assessment is a discussion about the future and how your organization will shape it. It is an intellectual and emotional adventure—for minds and hearts are involved. Rather than working in isolation, mission-driven social sector organizations, businesses, and government institutions with vision and new mind-sets will forge partnerships across all three sectors—the private, public, and social—to collaborate in building healthy communities. They will welcome the challenge of accountability; define and achieve meaningful results; and articulate their accomplishments in ways that draw interest, energy, and support to their mission. They will *change lives.*

The demand that social sector organizations (in fact, all organizations) show results is not a passing trend. Nor should it be. The demand today and for the future is *performance.* The first requirement of staff, volunteers, socially responsible businesses, and donors at all levels is to ensure that a difference is being made. They are asking, *How are you changing lives and communities for the better?* In this environment, self-assessment is vital.

If Peter Drucker were here to sit down with your organization, he would ask, *What is our mission? Who is our customer? What does the customer value? What are our results?* and *What is our plan?* He would ask these five questions because they go to the very heart of any organization—why it exists and how it will make a difference. They are The Five Most Important Questions because they are the *essential* questions.

One self-assessment participant called the questions "sharply pointed as a bayonet." The questions are not easy. By asking them, you will focus on excellence in performance and what you must do to achieve it. We, board and staff members of the Leader to Leader Institute, periodically ask the questions of ourselves, and we know when *you* ask these questions, all who participate in seeking answers will have an exuberant dialogue and conclusion.

This must be a *three-way* conversation that includes the board, the staff, and the customer. In the self-assessment process, we ask that you go directly to those you serve—your volunteers, your partners, your customers, and your supporters—and let their insights influence your own. How you think about results and how you innovate and change will be immeasurably enriched. When board and staff members, learning from their customers, shape their organization's mission and goals, they create an organizational focus with passion and energy behind it that carries the organization far beyond what one can imagine.

To be able to say "We are successful; we are furthering the mission," a social sector or a socially responsible organization must continuously appraise its performance. This revised and updated edition of the Leader to Leader Institute's *Self-Assessment Tool* is the result of such an appraisal. Since 1993, over 140,000 social sector leaders have purchased the *Self-Assessment Tool* for their organizations. Many leaders in all three sectors have written or spoken with us about their experience with Drucker's self-assessment process.

The feedback we have received is significant. We hear the *Tool* is a success, that using it indeed deepens an organization's sense of purpose and helps to define and achieve results. Our customers have told us they need more guidance in adapting the *Tool* to their particular setting, to streamline the *Participant Workbook,* to underscore the importance of listening to *their* customers, to clarify and sharpen the planning process, and to provide additional insights from Peter Drucker's philosophy on how to successfully implement a plan. And this is what we did. We are deeply grateful for the opportunity to learn from the ideas of those with on-the-ground experience and to respond to our valued customers.

We also have learned of the *Tool's* great flexibility. It is used by organizations in all three sectors. It is adapted and woven into a range of planning exercises for boards and management teams, project teams, and individuals. The *Tool* serves as a university-level teaching tool. And it is part of the reference libraries of executives in all three sectors. It is used by large and small organizations.

We welcome your use of the *Tool* however it best serves you. Please adapt the self-assessment process to the needs and culture of your organization. *Make it your own.*

The mission of the Leader to Leader Institute is to "strengthen the leadership of the social sector." We have no greater expression of this mission than the *Self-Assessment Tool*. The *Tool* is an adventure in organizational self-discovery, a means for assessing how to *be*—how to develop quality, character, values, and courage. It begins with questions and ends with action. To quote a customer, "It has only one purpose: to put the organization on track. And it works." On behalf of the Leader to Leader Institute, we welcome and encourage you on this journey into the future.

September 2010

Frances Hesselbein
President and Chief Executive Officer
Leader to Leader Institute
(founded as the Peter F. Drucker
Foundation for Nonprofit Management)

About Peter F. Drucker

Peter F. Drucker (1909–2005)—widely considered to be the world's foremost pioneer of management theory—was a writer, teacher, and consultant specializing in strategy and policy for businesses and social sector organizations. Drucker's career as a writer, consultant, and teacher spanned nearly seventy-five years. His groundbreaking work turned modern management theory into a serious discipline. He has influenced or created nearly every facet of its application, including decentralization, privatization, empowerment, and understanding of "the knowledge worker." He is the author of thirty-nine books, which have been translated into more than twenty languages. Thirteen books deal with society, economics, and politics; fifteen deal with management. Two of his books are novels, one is autobiographical, and he is coauthor of a book on Japanese painting. He has made four series of educational films based on his management books. He was an editorial columnist for the *Wall Street Journal* and a frequent contributor to the *Harvard Business Review* and other periodicals.

Drucker was born in 1909 in Vienna and was educated there and in England. He took his doctorate in public and international law while working as a newspaper reporter in Frankfurt, Germany. He then worked as an economist for an international bank in London. Drucker moved to London in 1933 to escape Hitler's Germany and took a job as a securities analyst for an insurance firm. Four years later, he married Doris Schmitz, and the couple departed for the United States in 1937.

Drucker landed a part-time teaching position at Sarah Lawrence College in New York in 1939. He joined the faculty of Bennington College in Vermont as professor of politics and philosophy in 1942, and the next year put his academic career on hold to spend two years studying the management structure of General Motors. This experience led to his book *Concept of the Corporation*, an immediate best-seller in the United States and Japan, which validated the notion that great companies could stand among humankind's noblest inventions. For more than twenty years, he was professor of management at the Graduate Business School of New York University. He was awarded the Presidential Citation, the university's highest honor.

Drucker came to California in 1971, where he was instrumental in the development of the country's first executive MBA program for working professionals at Claremont Graduate University (then known as Claremont Graduate School). The university's management school was named the Peter F. Drucker Graduate School of Management in his honor in 1987. He taught his last class at the school in the spring of 2002. His courses consistently attracted the largest number of students of any other class offered by the university.

As a consultant, Drucker specialized in strategy and policy for governments, businesses, and nonprofit organizations. His special focus was on the organization and work of top management. He worked with some of the world's largest businesses and with small and entrepreneurial companies. In recent years, he worked extensively with nonprofit organizations, including universities, hospitals, and churches. He served as a consultant to a number of agencies of the U.S. government and with the governments of Canada, Japan, Mexico, and other nations throughout the world.

Peter Drucker has been hailed in the United States and abroad as the seminal thinker, writer, and lecturer on the contemporary organization. Drucker's work has had a major influence on modern organizations and their management over the past sixty years. Valued for keen insight and the ability to convey his ideas in popular language, Drucker has often set the agenda in management thinking. Central to his philosophy is the view that people are an organization's most valuable resource and that a manager's job is to prepare and free people to perform. In 1997, he was featured on the cover of *Forbes* magazine under the headline "Still the Youngest Mind," and *Business Week* has called him "the most enduring management thinker of our time." On June 21, 2002, Peter Drucker received the Presidential Medal of Freedom from President George W. Bush.

Drucker received honorary doctorates from numerous universities around the world, including the United States, Belgium, Czechoslovakia, Great Britain, Japan, Spain, and Switzerland. He was honorary chairman of the Leader to Leader Institute from 1990 to 2002. He passed away on November 11, 2005, at age ninety-five.

How to Use This Workbook

Understanding Your Role

The *Self-Assessment Tool* was intentionally developed as a flexible resource. How you use the *Workbook* will depend on your setting and the particular purpose for which self-assessment is being conducted in your organization.

The *Workbook* may be in your hands because you have an interest in The Five Most Important Questions or because you have initiated or been invited by your organization's leadership to take part in self-assessment. You also may be part of a team selected to embark on this journey. Whatever the case, your experience and unique point of view will help your organization become more effective. Make sure that you understand your organization's overall focus of self-assessment and your role in the process. It is the responsibility of your organization's leadership to explain the purpose for self-assessment and to orient you in the process.

Introductory Workshop

If you are or will be attending an introductory workshop, your facilitator or group leader may have distributed the *Workbook* in advance. If you were not instructed to do so already, you are encouraged to read through the *Workbook* and review the worksheets, which you'll be working with in more depth during the workshop. If a facilitator assigned specific readings or worksheets, be sure to allow yourself sufficient time to complete this pre-work and digest the material. Doing so will make the time spent in the workshop or meeting more valuable. Be sure to bring the *Workbook* with you as well.

Prior to a workshop or when considering one, you may also want to read *The Five Most Important Questions You Will Ever Ask About Your Organization* (Jossey-Bass, 2008). This little book will orient you to Peter Drucker's essential questions and it provides insights from Jim Collins, Philip Kotler, Jim Kouzes, Judith Rodin, V. Kasturi Rangan, and Frances Hesselbein on the questions and on Drucker himself. If you are interested in conducting an introductory workshop, the *Facilitator's Guide* contains resources on how to design and lead half-day, full-day, and two-day workshops.

Organizational Self-Assessment

If you have been asked to participate in organizational self-assessment, you are a part of a strategic planning process that will help your organization revisit its mission, determine future direction, and develop a plan to achieve excellence in performance.

To help your organization explore Peter Drucker's Five Most Important Questions, you will use this *Participant Workbook* to (1) guide your individual thinking and (2) prepare for productive dialogue with other leaders in your organization. Dialogue sessions produce results-oriented strategic thinking and decision making.

Each chapter of the *Workbook* contains introductory passages from Peter Drucker, followed by worksheets you will use to explore each of The Five Most Important Questions. The passages are intended to help you understand self-assessment by providing theory, concepts, insight, and pertinent examples. Self-assessment is a framework for appraising performance and determining direction. *It is essential that you explore all of The Five Most Important Questions in the sequence they are presented.* At any point, you may revisit a question you have already examined.

Two copies of each worksheet are provided in this workbook so that if you attend an introductory workshop and write on the first copy, the second will be available should you need it during your self-assessment process.

Preparing for Facilitated Group Dialogue

Once you have familiarized yourself with self-assessment, you are ready to participate in a group discussion led by a facilitator. In group sessions, you will work with others in your organization to help assess its effectiveness and make recommendations for the future.

In a discussion group, there are no right or wrong answers. Participants are encouraged to agree or disagree freely with other members of the group, to change their minds, or to ask each other questions. When appropriate, a summary of the facilitated dialogue—including all areas discussed, agreements reached, decisions made, and next steps—will be compiled by the facilitator and presented to you or your organization's leadership for review. What is learned during self-assessment will be used to revisit the mission, determine direction, and take action.

Plan to spend at least one to two hours familiarizing yourself with the *Workbook* before you join your colleagues in facilitated dialogue. While you should review the worksheets for Question 5—"What Is Our Plan?"—they should not be completed until the organization is ready to revisit the mission, determine goals, and prepare the plan. If your organization selects worksheets for you to complete before your facilitated dialogue, please take enough time to do so. Although the workbook will not be collected, be sure to bring it with you to your group session or sessions, as it will serve as a helpful reference.

Understanding Self-Assessment Terms

This workbook uses Peter Drucker's core leadership and management principles and terminology. It is essential you use the terms during self-assessment—they will help you stay focused on results. Following are terms you will need to be familiar with before using this workbook. A glossary of additional terms can be found on p. 99.

Customer value   That which satisfies customers' needs (physical and psychological well-being), wants (where, when, and how a service or product is provided), and aspirations (desired future results).

Customers   Those who must be satisfied in order for the organization to achieve results. The *primary customer* is the person whose life is changed through the organization's work. *Supporting customers* are volunteers, members, partners, funders, referral sources, staff, and others who must be satisfied in order for the organization to achieve results.

Mission   The organization's reason for being, its purpose. Says what, in the end, the organization wants to be remembered for.

Results   The organization's bottom line. Defined in changed lives—behavior, circumstances, health, hopes, competence, or capacity. Results are always outside the organization.

Self-Assessment

The First Action Requirement of Leadership[1]

Editor's Note: This material and some of the proceeding sections authored by Peter Drucker are from the previous edition of the Participant Workbook. *Although some of the references and terminology are dated, Drucker's points and concepts are as relevant as ever to social sector organizations or to any organization with a socially driven mission.*

A Time to Shape the Future

Nonprofit institutions are central to the quality of life in America and central to citizenship; indeed, they carry the values of American society and the American tradition. The social sector organization has been America's resounding success in the last fifty years, whether we talk of institutions like the American Heart Association, which has taken leadership on major health issues; or of youth services such as the Girl Scouts of the U.S.A.; or of the recovery techniques of Alcoholics Anonymous; or of the fast-growing synagogues, churches, and mosques; or of the community developers that have revitalized urban neighborhoods; or of outstanding museums and colleges; or of the many other nonprofit groups that have emerged as the center of effective social action in a rapidly changing and turbulent America.

We are living through a period of sharp transformation. People born fifty years from now will not be able to imagine the world into which their own grandparents were born. Society is rearranging itself—its worldview, its basic values, its social and political structure, its arts, its key institutions. Social sector organizations will be needed even more urgently in the next decades as needs grow in two areas. First they will grow in what has traditionally been considered *charity*—helping the poor, the disabled, those who suffer deprivation, the victims of violence or disaster. And they will grow, perhaps even faster, in services that aim to *change the community and to change people.*

What new questions will arise and where the big new issues will lie, we can, I believe, already discover with some degree of probability. In many areas we can also describe what will not work. But answers to most questions are still largely hidden in the womb of the future. What the future society will look like depends on leaders in all sectors and on each of us in our work and life. This is a time to *shape the future*—precisely because everything is in flux. This is a time for self-assessment, a time for clear-minded decisions, and, above all, a time for action.

The Search for Community, Commitment, and Contribution

Every other American adult—90 million people all told—works at least three hours a week as "unpaid staff," that is, as a volunteer with a nonprofit organization. By the year 2010, the number of such unpaid staff people should have risen to 120 million, and their average hours of work to five per week. The main reason for this upsurge of volunteer participation in the United States is not the increase in need. The reason is the search for community, for commitment, and for contribution. Again and again when I talk to volunteers, I ask, "Why are you willing to give all this time when you are already working hard?" Again and again I get the same answer, "Because here I know what I am doing. Here I contribute. Here I am part of a community."

The nonprofit organization is a new center of meaningful citizenship, of active commitment. It offers the means to make a difference in one's community, one's society, one's own country, and beyond. Citizenship in and through the social sector is not a panacea for the world's ills, but it may be a prerequisite for tackling these ills. The organizations of the social sector have the critical leadership challenge to restore civic responsibility and the civic pride that is the mark of community.

Focus on Results

All social sector organizations share the common "bottom line" of *changed lives*. This is where *results* are—in the lives of people outside the organization—and achieving these bottom-line results is of absolute importance. Forty-five years ago, when I first began working with nonprofit organizations, many felt that good intentions were enough. "Business" subjects such as management, marketing, and return on investment were almost never discussed. Today, nonprofits have to think through very clearly what results are for their organization. They must demonstrate both commitment *and* competence in a highly demanding environment. People are no longer interested to know, "Is it a good cause?" Instead, they ask, "What is being achieved?

Is this a responsible organization worthy of my investment? What difference is being made in society, in this community, in the life of individuals?" The successful nonprofit institution will hold itself accountable for performance inside the organization—for effective marketing, for exemplary management of human and financial resources, for contribution in all areas—but always with the central focus on its one bottom line: changed lives.

The Five Most Important Questions

When we announced in 1990 that we were establishing the Peter F. Drucker Foundation for Nonprofit Management [now the Leader to Leader Institute], many in the social sector approached me, along with Frances Hesselbein and members of our board, saying, "The most important management resource we need is a method to help us think through what we are doing, why we are doing it, and what we *must* do." And so we developed this *Self-Assessment Tool,* which presents The Five Most Important Questions for any nonprofit organization to ask: *What is our mission? Who is our customer? What does the customer value? What are our results? What is our plan?*

The questions are straightforward—and deceptively simple. Throughout the self-assessment process, you will examine the fundamental question of your mission: what the mission is and what it *should* be. You will determine your *primary customer:* the person whose life is changed through your work. You will determine your *supporting customers:* volunteers, partners, donors, and others you must satisfy. You will engage in research to learn directly from customers what they value, decide what your results should be, and develop a plan with long-range goals and measurable objectives.

Encourage Constructive Dissent

All the first-rate decision makers I've observed had a very simple rule: If you have quick consensus on an important matter, don't make the decision. Acclamation means nobody has done the homework. The organization's decisions are important and risky, and they *should* be controversial. There is a very old saying—it goes back all the way to Aristotle and later became an axiom of the early Christian Church: In essentials unity, in action freedom, and in all things trust. Trust requires that dissent come out in the open.

Nonprofit institutions need a healthy atmosphere for dissent if they wish to foster innovation and commitment. Nonprofits must encourage honest and constructive disagreement precisely because everybody is committed to a good cause: your opinion versus mine can easily be taken as your good faith versus mine. Without proper encouragement, people have a tendency to avoid such difficult, but vital, discussions or turn them into underground feuds.

Another reason to encourage dissent is that any organization needs its nonconformist. This is not the kind of person who says, "There is a right way and a wrong way—and our way." Rather, he or she asks, "What is the right way *for the future?*" and is ready to change. Finally, open discussion uncovers what the objections are. With genuine participation, a decision doesn't need to be sold. Suggestions can be incorporated, objections addressed, and the decision itself becomes a commitment to action.

Creating Tomorrow's Society of Citizens

Your commitment to self-assessment is a commitment to developing yourself and your organization as a leader. You will expand your vision by listening to your customers, by encouraging constructive dissent, by looking at the sweeping transformation taking place in society. You have vital judgments ahead: whether to change the mission, whether to abandon programs that have outlived their usefulness and concentrate resources elsewhere, how to match opportunities with your competence and commitment, *how you will build community and change lives.* Self-assessment is the first action requirement of leadership: the constant resharpening, constant refocusing, never being really satisfied. And the time to do this is when you are successful. If you wait until things start to go down, then it's very difficult.

We are creating tomorrow's society of citizens through the social sector, through *your* nonprofit organization. And in that society, everybody is a leader, everybody is responsible, everybody acts. Therefore, mission and leadership are not just things to read about, to listen to; they are things to *do* something about. Self-assessment can and should convert good intentions and knowledge into effective action—not next year but tomorrow morning.

Peter F. Drucker

Question 1:
What Is Our Mission?

Worksheet 1.1:
What Is Our Current Mission?

Worksheet 1.2:
Does Our Mission Need to Be Revisited?

Worksheet 1.3:
What Are the Emerging Trends That Will Have the Greatest Impact?

Worksheet 1.4:
What Are Our Opportunities?

Question 2:
Who Is Our Customer?

Question 3:
What Does the Customer Value?

Question 4:
What Are Our Results?

Question 5:
What Is Our Plan?

Question 1:
What Is Our Mission?[2]

Each social sector institution exists to make a distinctive difference in the lives of individuals and in society. Making this difference is the mission—the organization's purpose and very reason for being. Each of more than one million nonprofit organizations in the United States may have a very different mission, but changing lives is always the starting point and ending point. A mission cannot be impersonal; it has to have deep meaning, be something you believe in—something you know is right. A fundamental responsibility of leadership is to make sure that everybody knows the mission, understands it, lives it.

Many years ago, I sat down with the administrators of a major hospital to think through the mission of the emergency room. As do most hospital administrators, they began by saying, "Our mission is health care." And that's the wrong definition. The hospital does not take care of health; the hospital takes care of illness. It took us a long time to come up with the very simple and (most people thought) too-obvious statement that the emergency room was there *to give assurance to the afflicted.* To do that well, you had to know what really went on. And, to the surprise of the physicians and nurses, the function of a good emergency room in their community was to tell eight out of ten people there was nothing wrong that a good night's sleep wouldn't fix. "You've been shaken up. Or the baby has the flu. All right, it's got convulsions, but there is nothing seriously wrong with the child." The doctors and nurses gave assurance.

We worked it out, but it sounded awfully obvious. Yet translating the mission into action meant that everybody who came in was seen by a qualified person in less than a minute. The first objective was to see everybody, almost immediately—because that is the only way to give assurance.

It Should Fit on a T-Shirt

The effective mission statement is short and sharply focused. It should fit on a T-shirt. The mission says *why* you do what you do, not the means by which you do it. The mission is broad, even eternal, yet directs you to do the right things now and into the future so that everyone in the organization can say, "What I am doing contributes to the goal." So it must be clear, and it must inspire. Every board member, volunteer, and staff person should be able to see the mission and say, "Yes. This is something I want to be remembered for."

To have an effective mission, you have to work out an exacting match of your opportunities, competence, and commitment. Every good mission statement reflects all three. You look first at the outside environment. The organization that starts from the inside and then tries to find places to put its resources is going to fritter itself away. Above all, it will focus on yesterday. Demographics change. Needs change. You must search out the accomplished facts—things that have already happened—that present challenges and opportunities for the organization. Leadership has no choice but to anticipate the future and attempt to mold it, bearing in mind that whoever is content to rise with the tide will also fall with it. It is not given to mortals to do any of these things well, but, lacking divine guidance, you must still assess where your opportunity lies.

Look at the state of the art, at changing conditions, at competition, the funding environment, at gaps to be filled. The hospital isn't going to sell shoes, and it's not going into education on a big scale. It's going to take care of the sick. But the specific aim may change. Things that are of primary importance now may become secondary or totally irrelevant very soon. With the limited resources you have—and I don't just mean people and money but also competence—where can you dig in and make a difference? Where can you set a new standard of performance? What really inspires your commitment?

Why Does the Organization Exist?

Defining the nonprofit mission is difficult, painful, and risky. But it alone enables you to set goals and objectives and go to work. Unless the mission is explicitly expressed, clearly understood, and supported by every member of the organization, the enterprise is at the mercy of events. Decision makers throughout will decide and act on the basis of different, incompatible, and conflicting ideas. They will pull in opposing directions without even being aware of their divergence, and your performance is what suffers. Common vision, understanding, and unity of direction and effort of the entire organization depend on defining the mission and what the mission *should* be.

Refining the Mission Statement[3]

Every three to five years, you should look at the mission again to decide whether it needs to be refocused because the demographics of your customers have changed, because you should abandon something that produces no results or needs resources beyond the organization's competencies, or because the objective has been accomplished.

You must think through priorities. That's easy to say, but to act on it is very hard because doing so always involves abandoning things that may look attractive, or giving up programs that people both inside and outside the organization are strongly encouraging you to keep. But if you don't concentrate your institution's resources, you are not going to get results. This may be the ultimate test of leadership: the ability to think through the priority decision and to make it stick.

Make Principled Decisions[4]

One cautionary note: *never subordinate the mission in order to get money.* If there are opportunities that threaten the integrity of the organization, you must say no. Otherwise, you sell your soul. I sat in on a discussion at a museum that had been offered a donation of important art on conditions that no self-respecting museum could possibly accept. Yet a few board members said, "Let's take the donation. We can change the conditions down the road." "No, that's unconscionable!" others responded, and the board fought over the issue. They finally agreed they would lose too much by compromising basic principles to please a donor. The board forfeited some very nice pieces of sculpture, but core values had to come first.

Keep Thinking It Through

Keep the central question, What is our mission? in front of you throughout the self-assessment process. Step by step you will analyze challenges and opportunities, identify your customers, learn what they value, and define your results. When it is time to develop the plan, you will take all that you have learned and revisit the mission to affirm or change it.

As you begin, consider this wonderful sentence from a sermon of that great poet and religious philosopher of the seventeenth century, John Donne: "Never start with tomorrow to reach eternity. Eternity is not being reached by small steps." We start with the long range and then feed back and say, "What do we do *today?*" The ultimate test is not the beauty of the mission statement. The ultimate test is your performance.

Peter F. Drucker

Worksheet 1.1:
What Is Our Current Mission?
(Workshop)

a. Write or attach a copy of the organization's mission statement here.

b. What is our organization's reason for being? Why do we do what we do?

c. What, in the end, do we want to be remembered for?

The Five Most Important Questions Self-Assessment Tool, Participant Workbook, Third Edition. Copyright © 2010 by Leader to Leader Institute. Reproduced by permission of Jossey-Bass, an Imprint of Wiley.

Worksheet 1.1:
What Is Our Current Mission?
(Organizational)

a. Write or attach a copy of the organization's mission statement here.

b. What is our organization's reason for being? Why do we do what we do?

c. What, in the end, do we want to be remembered for?

Worksheet 1.2:
Does Our Mission Need to Be Revisited?
(Workshop)

a. Rate the current mission using the following criteria and then decide if it should be revisited.

The Mission	Yes	To Some Extent	Not at All
Is short and focused—fits on a T-shirt	☐	☐	☐
Is clear and easily understood	☐	☐	☐
Defines purpose—why we do what we do, our reason for being	☐	☐	☐
Does not prescribe means	☐	☐	☐
Is sufficiently broad	☐	☐	☐
Inspires our commitment	☐	☐	☐
Says what, in the end, we want to be remembered for	☐	☐	☐

b. Should the mission be revisited?   ☐ Yes   ☐ No

If so, what changes should we consider?

Worksheet 1.2:
Does Our Mission Need to Be Revisited?
(Organizational)

a. Rate the current mission using the following criteria and then decide if it should be revisited.

The Mission	Yes	To Some Extent	Not at All
Is short and focused—fits on a T-shirt	☐	☐	☐
Is clear and easily understood	☐	☐	☐
Defines purpose—why we do what we do, our reason for being	☐	☐	☐
Does not prescribe means	☐	☐	☐
Is sufficiently broad	☐	☐	☐
Inspires our commitment	☐	☐	☐
Says what, in the end, we want to be remembered for	☐	☐	☐

b. Should the mission be revisited?   ☐ Yes   ☐ No

If so, what changes should we consider?

Worksheet 1.3:
What Are the Emerging Trends That Will Have the Greatest Impact?
(Workshop)

a. Identify emerging trends that will impact the organization. Describe the trend and note the data sources used to identify it (environmental scan, internal data, experience, and insight). Indicate if the trends will affect the organization in the short term, the long term, or both.*

Describe Trends	Note Data Sources
Changing demographics? ☐ Short Term ☐ Long Term	
Changing community conditions? ☐ Short Term ☐ Long Term	
Cultural or social trends? ☐ Short Term ☐ Long Term	

* *Short term* often is designated as one year; *long term* as three to five years.

The Five Most Important Questions Self-Assessment Tool, Participant Workbook, Third Edition. Copyright © 2010 by Leader to Leader Institute. Reproduced by permission of Jossey-Bass, an Imprint of Wiley.

Describe Trends   **Note Data Sources**

Economic trends; changes in the funding environment?
☐ Short Term   ☐ Long Term

Politics, legislation, or regulation?
☐ Short Term   ☐ Long Term

Media and communications?
☐ Short Term   ☐ Long Term

* *Short term* often is designated as one year; *long term* as three to five years.

Describe Trends	Note Data Sources

New models, methods, and technologies?
☐ Short Term   ☐ Long Term

Competition?
☐ Short Term   ☐ Long Term

Other?
☐ Short Term   ☐ Long Term

* *Short term* often is designated as one year; *long term* as three to five years.

b. What are the three to five trends that will have the greatest impact on our organization?

1.

2.

3.

4.

5.

Worksheet 1.3:
What Are the Emerging Trends That Will Have the Greatest Impact?
(Organizational)

a. Identify emerging trends that will impact the organization. Describe the trend and note the data sources used to identify it (environmental scan, internal data, experience, and insight). Indicate if the trends will affect the organization in the short term, the long term, or both.*

Describe Trends   **Note Data Sources**

Changing demographics?
    ☐ Short Term   ☐ Long Term

Changing community conditions?
    ☐ Short Term   ☐ Long Term

Cultural or social trends?
    ☐ Short Term   ☐ Long Term

* *Short term* often is designated as one year; *long term* as three to five years.

The Five Most Important Questions Self-Assessment Tool, Participant Workbook, Third Edition. Copyright © 2010 by Leader to Leader Institute. Reproduced by permission of Jossey-Bass, an Imprint of Wiley.

Describe Trends   **Note Data Sources**

Economic trends; changes in the funding environment?
☐ Short Term   ☐ Long Term

Politics, legislation, or regulation?
☐ Short Term   ☐ Long Term

Media and communications?
☐ Short Term   ☐ Long Term

* Short term often is designated as one year; long term as three to five years.

Describe Trends	Note Data Sources

New models, methods, and technologies?
☐ Short Term   ☐ Long Term

Competition?
☐ Short Term   ☐ Long Term

Other?
☐ Short Term   ☐ Long Term

* Short term often is designated as one year; *long term* as three to five years.

b. What are the three to five trends that will have the greatest impact on our organization?

1.

2.

3.

4.

5.

Worksheet 1.4:
What Are Our Opportunities?
(Workshop)

a. Refer to Worksheet 1.3, as well as other data sources (environmental scan, internal data, experience, and insight) to identify the organization's opportunities. Indicate if they are available in the short term, the long term, or both.*

1. What opportunities does the organization have to address compelling issues or conditions?

☐ Short Term
☐ Long Term

2. What opportunities does the organization have to fill a gap in its area of service?

☐ Short Term
☐ Long Term

3. What opportunities does the organization have to be a leader, to set a new standard of performance?

☐ Short Term
☐ Long Term

* *Short term* often is designated as one year; *long term* as three to five years.

4. What opportunities does the organization have to meet the interests of potential partners or funders?

☐ Short Term
☐ Long Term

5. Other opportunities:

☐ Short Term
☐ Long Term

* Short term often is designated as one year; *long term* as three to five years.

b. Which opportunities are the most promising for the organization? Why?

Worksheet 1.4:
What Are Our Opportunities?
(Organizational)

a. Refer to Worksheet 1.3, as well as other data sources (environmental scan, internal data, experience, and insight) to identify the organization's opportunities. Indicate if they are available in the short term, the long term, or both.*

---

1. What opportunities does the organization have to address compelling issues or conditions?

☐ Short Term
☐ Long Term

---

2. What opportunities does the organization have to fill a gap in its area of service?

☐ Short Term
☐ Long Term

---

3. What opportunities does the organization have to be a leader, to set a new standard of performance?

☐ Short Term
☐ Long Term

---

* *Short term* often is designated as one year; *long term* as three to five years.

---

4. What opportunities does the organization have to meet the interests of potential partners or funders?

☐ Short Term
☐ Long Term

5. Other opportunities:

☐ Short Term
☐ Long Term

* *Short term* often is designated as one year; *long term* as three to five years.

b. Which opportunities are the most promising for the organization? Why?

Question 1:
What Is Our Mission?

Question 2:
Who Is Our Customer?

Worksheet 2.1:
Who Are Our Primary and
Supporting Customers?

Worksheet 2.2:
How Will Our Customers Change?

Worksheet 2.3:
Are We Serving the Right Customers?

Question 3:
What Does the
Customer Value?

Question 4:
What Are Our Results?

Question 5:
What Is Our Plan?

Question 2
Who Is Our Customer?[5]

Not long ago, the word *customer* was rarely heard in the social sector. Nonprofit leaders would say, "We don't have customers. That's a marketing term. We have clients . . . recipients . . . patients. We have audience members. We have students." Rather than debate language, I ask, "Who must be satisfied for the organization to achieve results?" When you answer this question, you define your customer as one who values your service, who wants what you offer, who feels it's important to *them*.

Social sector organizations have two types of customers. The *primary customer* is the person whose life is changed through your work. Effectiveness requires focus, and that means *one* response to the question, Who is our primary customer? Those who chase off in too many directions suffer by diffusing their energies and diminishing their performance. *Supporting customers* are volunteers, members, partners, funders, referral sources, employees, and others who must be satisfied. They are all people who can say no, people who have the choice to accept or reject what you offer. You might satisfy them by providing the opportunity for meaningful service, by directing contributions toward results you both believe in, by joining forces to meet community needs.

The primary customer is never the *only* customer, and to satisfy one customer without satisfying the others means there is no performance. This makes it very tempting to say there is more than one primary customer, but effective organizations resist this temptation and keep to a focus—the primary customer.

Identify the Primary Customer

Let me give you a positive example of identifying and concentrating on the primary customer in a complex setting. A mid-sized nonprofit organization's mission is *to increase people's economic and social independence.* They have twenty-five programs considered to be in four different fields, but for thirty-five years they have focused on only one primary customer: *the person with multiple barriers to employment.* In the beginning, this meant the physically handicapped. Today, it still means people with disabilities but also single mothers who want to be finished with welfare, older workers who have been laid off, people with chronic and persistent mental illness living in the community, and those struggling against long-term chemical dependency. Each belongs to a single primary customer group: the person with multiple barriers to employment. Results are measured in every program by whether the customer can now gain and keep productive work.

The primary customer is not necessarily someone you can reach, someone you can sit down with and talk to directly. Primary customers may be infants, or endangered species, or members of a future generation. Whether or not you can have an active dialogue, identifying the primary customer puts your priorities in order and gives you a reference point for critical decisions on the organization's values.

Identify Supporting Customers

The Girl Scouts of the U.S.A. is the largest girls' and women's organization in the world and a nonprofit that exemplifies service to one primary customer—the girl—balanced with satisfaction of many supporting customers, all of whom change over time. A long-held Girl Scouts priority is offering equal access to every girl in the United States. This has not changed since 1912, when the Girl Scouts founder said, "I have something for all the girls." Frances Hesselbein, at the time she was national executive director (1976–1990), told me, "We look at the projections and understand that by the year 2000, one-third of this country will be members of minority groups. Many people are very apprehensive about the future and what this new racial and ethnic composition will mean. We see it as an unprecedented opportunity to reach all girls with a program that will help them in their growing-up years, which are more difficult than ever before."

Reaching a changing primary customer means a new view of supporting customers. Frances explained, "In a housing project with no Girl Scout troop there are hundreds of young girls really needing this kind of program, and families wanting something better for their children. It is important as we reach out to girls in every racial and economic group to understand the very special needs, the culture, the readiness of each group. We work with many supporting customers; with the clergy perhaps, with the director of that housing project, with parents—a group of people from that particular community. We recruit leaders, train them right there. We have to demonstrate our respect for that community, our interest in it. Parents have to know it will be a positive experience for their daughters."

Know Your Customers

Customers are never static. There will be greater or lesser numbers in the groups you already serve. They will become more diverse. Their needs, wants, and aspirations will evolve. There may be entirely new customers you must satisfy to achieve results—individuals who really need the service, want the service, but not in the way in which it is available today. And there are customers you should *stop* serving because the organization has filled a need, because people can be better served elsewhere, or because you are not producing results.

Answering the question, Who is our customer? provides the basis for determining what customers value, defining your results, and developing the plan. Yet, even after careful thought, customers may surprise you; then you must be prepared to adjust. I remember one of my pastoral friends saying of a new program, "Great, a wonderful program for the newly married." The program was indeed a success. But to the consternation of the young assistant pastor who designed it and ran it, not a single newly married couple enrolled. All the participants were young people living together and wondering whether they should get married. And the senior pastor had a terrible time with his brilliant young assistant, who became righteous and said, "We haven't designed it for them!" He wanted to throw them out.

Often, the customer is one step ahead of you. So you must *know your customer*—or quickly get to know them. Time and again you will have to ask, "Who is our customer?" because customers constantly change. The organization that is devoted to results—always with regard for its basic integrity—will adapt and change as they do.

Peter F. Drucker

Worksheet 2.1: Who Are Our Primary and Supporting Customers? (Workshop)

a. *Who is our primary customer?* The primary customer is the person whose life is changed through the organization's work.

b. *Who are our supporting customers?* Identify who, in addition to the primary customer, must be satisfied in order for the organization to achieve results.

Worksheet 2.1:
Who Are Our Primary and Supporting Customers?
(Organizational)

a. *Who is our primary customer?* The primary customer is the person whose life is changed through the organization's work.

b. *Who are our supporting customers?* Identify who, in addition to the primary customer, must be satisfied in order for the organization to achieve results.

Worksheet 2.2:
How Will Our Customers Change?
(Workshop)

Think about how the organization's customers will change for each of the following characteristics. Indicate if the customer will change and briefly describe the anticipated change.

a. How will our *primary customer* change in the next three to five years?

Number: (greater or fewer) ☐ Yes ☐ No

Demographics: (age, race, and so on) ☐ Yes ☐ No

Needs, wants, and aspirations: ☐ Yes ☐ No

Other: ☐ Yes ☐ No

b. What are the implications of these changes for our organization?

---

c. How will our *supporting customers* change in the next three to five years? For each supporting customer identified in Worksheet 2.1, identify and describe anticipated changes. If necessary, make duplicates of this worksheet for each supporting customer.

Supporting Customer:

Number: (greater or fewer)　　　　　☐ Yes　　☐ No

Demographics: (age, race, and so on)　　☐ Yes　　☐ No

Needs, wants, and aspirations:　　　　☐ Yes　　☐ No

Other:　　　　　　　　　　　　　　☐ Yes　　☐ No

d. What are the implications of these changes for our organization?

Think about how the organization's customers will change for each of the following characteristics. Indicate if the customer will change and briefly describe the anticipated change.

a. How will our *primary customer* change in the next three to five years?

Number: (greater or fewer) ☐ Yes ☐ No

Demographics: (age, race, and so on) ☐ Yes ☐ No

Needs, wants, and aspirations: ☐ Yes ☐ No

Other: ☐ Yes ☐ No

b. What are the implications of these changes for our organization?

c. How will our *supporting customers* change in the next three to five years? For each supporting customer identified in Worksheet 2.1, identify and describe anticipated changes. If necessary, make duplicates of this worksheet for each supporting customer.

Supporting Customer:

Number: (greater or fewer) ☐ Yes ☐ No

Demographics: (age, race, and so on) ☐ Yes ☐ No

Needs, wants, and aspirations: ☐ Yes ☐ No

Other: ☐ Yes ☐ No

d. What are the implications of these changes for our organization?

Worksheet 2.3:
Are We Serving the Right Customers? (Workshop)

a. Are there potential new customers we must satisfy to further the mission?

☐ Yes   ☐ No

b. If so, who are they? Why should the organization start serving them?

c. Are there existing customers we should stop serving because the organization has satisfied a need, those customers can be better served elsewhere, or we are not producing results?

☐ Yes   ☐ No

d. If so, who are they? Why should the organization stop serving them?

Worksheet 2.3:
Are We Serving the Right Customers?
(Organizational)

a. Are there potential new customers we must satisfy to further the mission?

☐ Yes   ☐ No

b. If so, who are they? Why should the organization start serving them?

c. Are there existing customers we should stop serving because the organization has satisfied a need, those customers can be better served elsewhere, or we are not producing results?

☐ Yes   ☐ No

d. If so, who are they? Why should the organization stop serving them?

Question 1:
What Is Our Mission?

Question 2:
Who Is Our Customer?

Question 3:
What Does the
Customer Value?

Worksheet 3.1:
What Do Our Customers Value?

Worksheet 3.2:
What Knowledge Do We Need
to Gain from Our Customers?

Worksheet 3.3:
How Will We Gather Information?

Question 4:
What Are Our Results?

Question 5:
What Is Our Plan?

Question 3:

What Does the Customer Value?[6]

The question, What do customers value?—what satisfies their needs, wants, and aspirations—is so complicated that it can only be answered by customers themselves. And the first rule is that there are no irrational customers. Almost without exception, customers behave rationally in terms of their own realities and their own situation. Leadership should not even try to guess at the answers but should always go to the customers in a systematic quest for those answers. I practice this. Each year I personally telephone a random sample of fifty or sixty students who graduated ten years earlier. I ask, "Looking back, what did we contribute in this school? What is still important to you? What should we do better? What should we stop doing?" And believe me, the knowledge I have gained has had a profound influence.

What does the customer value? may be the most important question. Yet it is the one least often asked. Nonprofit leaders tend to answer it for themselves. "It's the quality of our programs. It's the way we improve the community." People are so convinced they are doing the right things and so committed to their cause that they come to see the institution as an end in itself. But that's a bureaucracy. Instead of asking, "Does it deliver value to our customers?" they ask, "Does it fit our rules?" And that not only inhibits performance but also destroys vision and dedication.

Understand Your Assumptions

My friend Philip Kotler, a professor at Northwestern University, points out that many organizations are very clear about the value they would like to deliver, but they often don't understand that value from the perspective of their customers. They make assumptions based on their own interpretation. So begin with assumptions and find out what *you* believe your customers value. Then you can compare these beliefs with what customers actually are saying, find the differences, and go on to assess your results.

What Does the Primary Customer Value?

Learning what their primary customers value led to significant change in a homeless shelter. The shelter's existing beliefs about value added up to nutritious meals and clean beds. A series of face-to-face interviews with their homeless customers was arranged, and both board and staff members took part. They found out that yes, the food and beds are appreciated but do little or nothing to satisfy the deep aspiration *not to be homeless*. The customers said, "We need a place of safety from which to rebuild our lives, a place we can at least temporarily call a real home." The organization threw out their assumptions and their old rules. They said, "How can we make this shelter a safe haven?" They eliminated the fear that comes with being turned back on the street each morning. They now make it possible to stay at the shelter quite a while, and work with individuals to find out what a rebuilt life means to them and how they can be helped to realize their goal.

The new arrangement also requires more of the customer. Before, it was enough to show up hungry. Now, to get what the customer values most, he must make a commitment. He must work on his problems and plans in order to stay on. The customer's stake in the relationship is greater, as are the organization's results.

What Do Supporting Customers Value?

Your knowledge of what primary customers value is of utmost importance. Yet the reality is, unless you understand equally what supporting customers value, you will not be able to put all the necessary pieces in place for the organization to perform. In social sector organizations there have always been a multitude of supporting customers, in some cases each with a veto power. A school principal has to satisfy teachers, the school board, community partners, the taxpayers, parents, and above all, the primary customer—the young student. The principal has six constituencies, each of which sees the school differently. Each of them is essential, each defines value differently, and each has to be satisfied at least to the point where they don't fire the principal, go on strike, or rebel.

What Will Encourage Contributors?

Knowing what supporting customers value enables nonprofit institutions to address two of today's biggest challenges. The first is to convert individuals who give money into "contributors," that is, citizens who take responsibility, neighbors who care.

Philip Kotler reminds us that this requires careful identification of the appropriate sources of funds and the giving motives. What are that individual's personal reasons for giving money? To whom does he or she give? What results prompt the contributor to say, "Yes, that's what should be done. That's what deserves more of my support"? What does this customer value enough to do more, to really become a partner in furthering the mission?

What Does "Making a Difference" Mean to Each Volunteer?

Then there is the second major challenge for nonprofits: to enhance community and common purpose. What nonprofits do for their volunteers may well be as important as what they do for their primary customers. The reason is that volunteers search for opportunities to make a meaningful contribution. They feel the need to do something where "I can make a difference." But again, you must discover what "making a difference" means to each volunteer and how they must be satisfied in order for them to give their commitment.

Listen to Your Customers

To formulate a successful plan you will need to understand each of your constituencies' concerns, especially what they consider results in the long term. Integrating what customers value into the institution's plan is almost an architectural process, a structural process. It's not too difficult to do once it's understood, but it's hard work. First, think through what knowledge you need to gain. Then listen to customers, accept what they value as objective fact, and make sure the customer's voice is part of your discussions and decisions, not just during this self-assessment process, but continually.

Peter F. Drucker

Worksheet 3.1:
What Do Our Customers Value?
(Workshop)

This worksheet focuses on the existing data the organization uses to understand what the customer values. Worksheets 3.2 and 3.3 focus on the data the organization needs to gather—and how to gather it.

a. Describe what the *primary customer* values (that which satisfies customer needs, wants, and aspirations). Indicate the data sources for each point listed: environmental scan, customer research, experience, and insight.

What does the customer value?	Note Data Sources
Primary customer:	

The Five Most Important Questions Self-Assessment Tool, Participant Workbook, Third Edition. Copyright © 2010 by Leader to Leader Institute. Reproduced by permission of Jossey-Bass, an Imprint of Wiley.

b. Describe what each *supporting customer* values. Indicate the data sources: environmental scan, customer research, experience, and insight. If necessary, make duplicates of this worksheet for each supporting customer.

What does the customer value?	Note Data Sources
Supporting customer:	
Supporting customer:	

c. Describe what each *potential new customer* values. Indicate the data sources: environmental scan, customer research, experience, and insight. If necessary, make duplicates of this worksheet for each potential new customer.

What does the customer value?	Note Data Sources

Potential new customer:

Potential new customer:

Worksheet 3.1:
What Do Our Customers Value?
(Organizational)

This worksheet focuses on the existing data the organization uses to understand what the customer values. Worksheets 3.2 and 3.3 focus on the data the organization needs to gather—and how to gather it.

a. Describe what the *primary customer* values (that which satisfies customer needs, wants, and aspirations). Indicate the data sources for each point listed: environmental scan, customer research, experience, and insight.

What does the customer value?	Note Data Sources
Primary customer:	

Worksheet 3.1:
What Do Our Customers Value? (cont'd)
(Organizational)

b. Describe what each *supporting customer* values. Indicate the data sources: environmental scan, customer research, experience, and insight. If necessary, make duplicates of this worksheet for each supporting customer.

What does the customer value?	Note Data Sources
Supporting customer:	
Supporting customer:	

c. Describe what each *potential new customer* values. Indicate the data sources: environmental scan, customer research, experience, and insight. If necessary, make duplicates of this worksheet for each potential new customer.

What does the customer value?	Note Data Sources
Potential new customer:	
Potential new customer:	

Worksheet 3.2:
What Knowledge Do We Need to Gain from Our Customers?
(Workshop)

Listening to the customer is indispensable. The organization's understanding about its customers may be confirmed or significantly altered when it listens to the customer. Imagine the organization has the opportunity to ask its customers any question. What knowledge is needed to understand what the customer values?

Customer	Knowledge We Need
Primary customer:	

Customer	Knowledge We Need
Supporting customers:	
1.	
2.	
3.	
4.	
Other:	

Customer	Knowledge We Need

Potential new customers:

1.

2.

3.

Worksheet 3.2:
What Knowledge Do We Need to
Gain from Our Customers?
(Organizational)

Listening to the customer is indispensable. The organization's understanding about its customers may be confirmed or significantly altered when it listens to the customer. Imagine the organization has the opportunity to ask its customers any question. What knowledge is needed to understand what the customer values?

Customer	Knowledge We Need
Primary customer:	

Worksheet 3.2:
What Knowledge Do We Need to Gain from Our Customers? (cont'd) (Organizational)

Customer	Knowledge We Need
Supporting customers:	
1.	
2.	
3.	
4.	
Other:	

Customer	Knowledge We Need

Potential new customers:

1.

2.

3.

Worksheet 3.3:
How Will We Gather Information?
(Workshop)

Use Worksheet 3.2 and identify the best ways to collect the knowledge the organization needs to understand what its customers value. Methods may include customer surveys, focus groups, interviews, and feedback instruments.

Knowledge We Need	Data-Collection Method(s)
1.	
2.	
3.	
4.	
5.	

The Five Most Important Questions Self-Assessment Tool, Participant Workbook, Third Edition. Copyright © 2010 by Leader to Leader Institute. Reproduced by permission of Jossey-Bass, an Imprint of Wiley.

Worksheet 3.3:
How Will We Gather Information?
(Organizational)

Use Worksheet 3.2 and identify the best ways to collect the knowledge the organization needs to understand what its customers value. Methods may include customer surveys, focus groups, interviews, and feedback instruments.

Knowledge We Need	Data-Collection Method(s)
1.	
2.	
3.	
4.	
5.	

Question 1:
What Is Our Mission?

Question 2:
Who Is Our Customer?

Question 3:
What Does the
Customer Value?

Question 4:
What Are Our Results?

Worksheet 4.1:
How Do We Define Results?

Worksheet 4.2:
How Do We Measure Results?

Worksheet 4.3:
How Can We Improve Our Performance?

Question 5:
What Is Our Plan?

Question 4:
What Are Our Results?[7]

The results of social sector organizations are always measured *outside* the organization in changed lives and changed conditions—in people's behavior, circumstances, health, hopes, and, above all, their competence and capacity. To further the mission, each nonprofit needs to determine what should be appraised and judged, then concentrate resources for results.

Look at Short-Term Accomplishments and Long-Term Change

A small mental health center was founded and directed by a dedicated husband-and-wife team, both psychotherapists. They called it a "healing community," and in the fifteen years they ran the organization, they achieved results others had dismissed as impossible. Their primary customers were people diagnosed with schizophrenia, and most came to the center following failure after failure in treatment, their situation nearly hopeless.

The people at the center said, "There *is* somewhere to turn." Their first measure was whether primary customers and their families were willing to try again. The staff had a number of ways to monitor progress. Did participants regularly attend group sessions and participate fully in daily routines? Did the incidence and length of psychiatric hospitalizations decrease? Could these individuals show new understanding of their disease by saying, "I have had an episode," as opposed to citing demons in the closet? As they progressed, could participants set realistic goals for their own next steps?

The center's mission was *to enable people with serious and persistent mental illness to recover,* and after two or more years of intensive work, many could function in this world—they were no longer "incurable." Some were able to return to a life with their family. Others could hold steady jobs. A few completed graduate school. Whether or not members of that healing community did recover—whether the lives of primary customers changed in this fundamental way—was the organization's single bottom line.

In business, you can debate whether profit is really an adequate measuring stick, but without it, there is no business in the long term. In the social sector, no such universal standard for success exists. Each organization must identify its customers, learn what they value, develop meaningful measures, and honestly judge whether, in fact, lives are being changed. This is a new discipline for many nonprofit groups, but it is one that can be learned.

How *Should* the Organization Define Results?

What should be measured and monitored? What are the meaningful criteria for us? What are the prerequisites for success? These are the questions most often raised when I work with social sector organizations to define results. To decide, you return to the mission. You take into account your capabilities, the environment in which you work, the best studies and examples in your field. You listen carefully to primary customers and apply your knowledge of who they are and what they value. You think qualitatively and quantitatively. You work through this discipline until you are resolved on the bottom line and can therefore determine what in your organization must be appraised and judged.

Table 1 shows three examples of decisions on what results should be.

TABLE 1. EXAMPLES OF RESULTS.

Mission: To prevent the spread of AIDS	*Results:* 1. Attitude shifts from "AIDS is something that happens to other people" to acceptance of personal responsibility. 2. People in targeted population groups change their sexual behavior. 3. The number of new cases of AIDS drops.
Mission (for a school): To develop contributing citizens	*Results:* 1. Students are constructive team members and respectful in peer relationships. 2. Graduates go on to advanced education or make a smooth transition to employment. 3. Graduates are active citizens who make a difference in their communities or beyond.

Mission (for a United Way): To improve lives by mobilizing the caring power of communities around the world to advance the common good *Note:* taken from United Way website, http://www.liveunited.org/about/missvis.cfm	*Results:* 1. The most vulnerable are safe and supported. 2. Human services are well resourced and co-operatively strengthen communities, families, and individuals. 3. Economic and social disparities are reduced. 4. Priority community problems and issues are identified and overcome.

Qualitative and Quantitative Measures

Progress and achievement can be appraised in *qualitative* and *quantitative* terms. These two types of measures are interwoven—they shed light on one another—and both are necessary to illuminate in what ways and to what extent lives are being changed.

Qualitative measures address the depth and breadth of change within its particular context. They begin with specific observations, build toward patterns, and tell a subtle, individualized story. Qualitative appraisal offers valid, "rich" data. The education director at a major museum tells of the man who sought her out to explain how the museum had opened his teenage mind to new possibilities in a way he knew literally saved his life. She used this result to support her inspiration for a new initiative with troubled youth. The people in a successful research institute cannot quantify the value of their research ahead of time. But they can sit down every three years and ask, "What have we achieved that contributed to changed lives? Where do we focus now for results tomorrow?" Qualitative results can be in the realm of the intangible, such as instilling hope in a patient battling cancer. Qualitative data, although sometimes more subjective and difficult to grasp, are just as real, just as important, and can be gathered just as systematically as the quantitative.

Quantitative measures use definitive standards. They begin with categories and expectations and tell an objective story. Quantitative appraisal offers valid "hard" data. Examples of quantitative measures are as follows: whether overall school performance improves when at-risk youth have intensive arts education; whether the percentage of welfare recipients who complete training and become employed at a livable wage goes up; whether health professionals change their practice based on new research; whether the number of teenagers who smoke goes up or down; whether incidences of child abuse fall when twenty-four-hour crisis care is available.

Quantitative measures are essential for assessing whether resources are properly concentrated for results, whether progress is being made, whether lives and communities are changing for the better.

Concentrate Resources for Success

Success is realized through concentration, not by splintering. That enormous organization the Salvation Army concentrates on only four or five programs. Its executives have the courage to say, "This is not for us. Other people do it better" or "This is not where we can make the greatest contribution. It does not really fit the strength we have." Success is judged, for example, by the percentage of alcoholics restored to mental and physical health, the number of offenders who stay out of prison, how quickly and completely food kitchens and temporary shelters provide relief at the scene of a disaster.

The most exciting thing to me in almost fifty years of work with nonprofit organizations is that we no longer talk of the *need* but of success in achieving results. To believe that whatever we do is a moral cause and should be pursued whether there is success or not is a perennial temptation for nonprofit executives—and even more for their boards. Everything is "the Lord's work" or "a good cause," but we cannot afford to continue where we seem unable to further the mission. There are exceptions—those who labor in the wilderness, the true believers who are devoted to a cause and to whom success, failure, and results are irrelevant. We need such people. They are our conscience. But very few of them achieve. Nonprofit organizations are asking, "Have we been successful?" and it's high time they did.

Assess What Must Be Strengthened or Abandoned

One of the most important questions for nonprofit leadership is, Do we produce results that are sufficiently outstanding for us to justify putting our resources in this area? Need alone does not justify continuing. Nor does tradition. You must match your mission, your concentration, and your results. Like the New Testament parable of the talents, your job is to invest your resources where the returns are manifold, where you can have success.

To abandon anything is always bitterly resisted. People in any organization are always attached to the obsolete—the things that should have worked but did not, the things that once were productive and no longer are. They are most attached to what in an earlier book (*Managing for Results,* 1964) I called "investments in managerial ego." Yet abandonment comes first. Until that has been accomplished, little else gets done. The acrimonious and emotional debate over what to abandon holds everybody in its grip. Abandoning anything is thus difficult, but only for a fairly short spell. Rebirth can begin once the dead are buried; six months later, everybody wonders, "Why did it take us so long?"

Leadership Is Accountable

If essential performance areas are weak, they must be strengthened. But even then, you must consider "the unthinkable." In one international nonprofit I know of, a highly successful training program had, over thirty years, made a profound difference in health care practices for an entire nation. With an elaborate trans-Pacific infrastructure in place—and a handsome but overly specific endowment supporting it—today's leadership had to address the fact that the training strategy could no longer make a difference for the future and to begin dismantling it in favor of unproved innovations.

There are times to face the fact that the organization as a whole is not performing—that there are weak results everywhere and little prospect of improving. It may be time to merge or to liquidate and put your energies somewhere else. And in some performance areas, whether to strengthen or abandon is not clear. You will need a systematic analysis as part of your plan.

At this point in the self-assessment process, you determine what results for the organization should be and where to concentrate for future success. The mission defines the scope of your responsibility. Leadership is accountable to determine what must be appraised and judged, to protect the organization from squandering resources, and to ensure meaningful results.

Peter F. Drucker

Worksheet 4.1:
How Do We Define Results?
(Workshop)

Results are measured *outside* the organization in the form of changed lives. After exploring the first three questions on mission, customer, and value, how do we define results?

Result:

Result:

Result:

Result:

Worksheet 4.1:
How Do We Define Results?
(Organizational)

Results are measured *outside* the organization in the form of changed lives. After exploring the first three questions on mission, customer, and value, how do we define results?

Result:

Result:

Result:

Result:

The Five Most Important Questions Self-Assessment Tool, Participant Workbook, Third Edition. Copyright © 2010 by Leader to Leader Institute. Reproduced by permission of Jossey-Bass, an Imprint of Wiley.

Worksheet 4.2:
How Do We Measure Results?
(Workshop)

How do we measure our progress and achievement for each result we identified in Worksheet 4.1?

	Quantitative Measures	Qualitative Measures
Result:		
Result:		
Result:		
Result:		

Worksheet 4.2:
How Do We Measure Results?
(Organizational)

How do we measure our progress and achievement for each result we identified in Worksheet 4.1?

	Quantitative Measures	Qualitative Measures
Result:		
Result:		
Result:		
Result:		

Worksheet 4.3: How Can We Improve Our Performance? (Workshop)

a. How do we concentrate our efforts? List each of the organization's programs and identify if it is strong and can produce greater results; if it is weak and in need of improvement; or if it is a candidate for planned abandonment. Explain why.

Programs

1.

☐ Strong/Growth Area
☐ Weak/Needs Improvement
☐ Abandon

2.

☐ Strong/Growth Area
☐ Weak/Needs Improvement
☐ Abandon

3.

☐ Strong/Growth Area
☐ Weak/Needs Improvement
☐ Abandon

4.

☐ Strong/Growth Area
☐ Weak/Needs Improvement
☐ Abandon

5.

☐ Strong/Growth Area
☐ Weak/Needs Improvement
☐ Abandon

b. Innovation is "change that creates a new dimension of performance." Do we have any opportunities for innovation? If yes, what are they?

c. How well do our internal systems support program performance and innovation? Identify what is strong, what is weak, and what needs to be analyzed.

Internal Systems		Analyze (describe)
Human resource management	☐ Strong ☐ Weak	
Finance/Budget	☐ Strong ☐ Weak	
Development/Fundraising	☐ Strong ☐ Weak	
Marketing, communications, public relations	☐ Strong ☐ Weak	
Quality assurance	☐ Strong ☐ Weak	
Board development	☐ Strong ☐ Weak	
Information technology	☐ Strong ☐ Weak	

a. How do we concentrate our efforts? List each of the organization's programs and identify if it is strong and can produce greater results; if it is weak and in need of improvement; or if it is a candidate for planned abandonment. Explain why.

Programs

1. _____

☐ Strong/Growth Area
☐ Weak/Needs Improvement
☐ Abandon

2. _____

☐ Strong/Growth Area
☐ Weak/Needs Improvement
☐ Abandon

3. _____

☐ Strong/Growth Area
☐ Weak/Needs Improvement
☐ Abandon

4. _____

☐ Strong/Growth Area
☐ Weak/Needs Improvement
☐ Abandon

5. _____

☐ Strong/Growth Area
☐ Weak/Needs Improvement
☐ Abandon

b. Innovation is "change that creates a new dimension of performance." Do we have any opportunities for innovation? If yes, what are they?

c. How well do our internal systems support program performance and innovation? Identify what is strong, what is weak, and what needs to be analyzed.

Internal Systems		Analyze (describe)
Human resource management	☐ Strong ☐ Weak	
Finance/Budget	☐ Strong ☐ Weak	
Development/Fundraising	☐ Strong ☐ Weak	
Marketing, communications, public relations	☐ Strong ☐ Weak	
Quality assurance	☐ Strong ☐ Weak	
Board development	☐ Strong ☐ Weak	
Information technology	☐ Strong ☐ Weak	

Question 1:
What Is Our Mission?

Question 2:
Who Is Our Customer?

Question 3:
What Does the
Customer Value?

Question 4:
What Are Our Results?

Question 5:
What Is Our Plan?

Worksheet 5.1:
What Is Our Mission?

Worksheet 5.2:
What Are Our Goals?

Worksheet 5.3:
What Is Our Plan to Achieve
Results for the Organization?

Worksheet 5.4:
How Will We Communicate Our
Mission, Plan, and Results?

Question 5: What Is Our Plan?[8]

Get the Right Things Done

The self-assessment process leads to a plan that is a concise summation of the organization's purpose and future direction. The plan encompasses mission, vision, goals, objectives, action steps, a budget, and appraisal. Now comes the point to affirm or change the mission and set long-range goals. Remember, every mission statement has to reflect three things: opportunities, competence, and commitment. It answers the questions, *What is our purpose? Why do we do what we do? What, in the end, do we want to be remembered for?* The mission transcends today but guides today, informs today. It provides the framework for setting goals and mobilizing the resources of the organization for getting the right things done.

The development and formal adoption of mission and goals are fundamental to effective governance of a nonprofit organization and are primary responsibilities of the board. Therefore, these strategic elements of the plan must be approved by the board.

To further the mission, there must be action today and specific aims for tomorrow. Yet planning is not masterminding the future. Any attempt to do so is foolish; the future is unpredictable. In the face of uncertainties, planning defines the particular place you *want* to be and how you intend to get there. Planning does not substitute facts for judgment nor science for leadership. It recognizes the importance of analysis, courage, experience, intuition—even hunch. It is responsibility rather than technique.

Goals Are Few, Overarching, and Approved by the Board

The most difficult challenge is to agree on the institution's goals—the fundamental long-range direction. Goals are overarching and should be few in number. If you have more than five goals, you have none. You're simply spreading yourself too thin. Goals make it absolutely clear where you will concentrate resources for results—the mark of an organization serious about success. Goals flow from mission, aim the organization where it must go, build on strength, address opportunity, and, taken together, outline your desired future.

An option for the plan is a vision statement picturing a future when the organization's goals are achieved and its mission accomplished. The Leader to Leader Institute's vision is, "to chart the future path for the social sector to become the equal partner of business and government in developing responsible leaders, caring citizens, and a healthy, diverse and inclusive society." I have worked with groups who became intensely motivated by these often idealistic and poetic statements, whereas others say, "Let's not get carried away." If a vision statement—whether a sentence or a page—helps bring the plan to life, by all means include it.

Here is an example of the vision, mission, and goals for an art museum.

Vision	A city where the world's diverse artistic heritage is prized and whose people seek out art to feed their minds and spirits
Mission	To bring art and people together
Goal 1	To conserve the collections and inspire partnerships to seek and acquire exceptional objects
Goal 2	To enable people to discover, enjoy, and understand art through popular and scholarly exhibitions, community education, and publications
Goal 3	To significantly expand the museum's audience and strengthen its impact with new and traditional members
Goal 4	To maintain state-of-the-art facilities, technologies, and operations
Goal 5	To enhance long-term financial security

Building around mission and long-term goals is the only way to integrate shorter-term interests. Then management can always ask, "Is an objective leading us toward our basic long-range goal, or is it going to sidetrack us, divert us, make us lose sight of our aims?" St. Augustine said, "One prays for miracles but works for results." Your plan leads you to work for results. It converts intentions into action.

Objectives Are Measurable, Concrete, and the Responsibility of Management

Objectives are the specific and measurable levels of achievement that move the organization toward its goals. The chief executive officer is responsible for development of objectives and the action steps and detailed budgets that follow. The board must not act at the level of tactical planning, or it interferes with management's vital ability to be flexible in how goals are achieved. When developing and implementing a plan, the board is accountable for mission, goals, and the allocation of resources to results, and for appraising progress and achievement. Management is accountable for objectives, for action steps, for the supporting budget, as well as for demonstrating effective performance.

Five Elements of Effective Plans

Abandonment

The first decision is whether to abandon what does not work, what has never worked—the things that have outlived their usefulness and their capacity to contribute. Ask of any program, system, or customer group, "If we were not committed to this today, would we go into it?" If the answer is no, say, "How can we get out—fast?"

Concentration

Concentration is building on success, strengthening what *does* work. The best rule is to put your efforts into your successes. You will get maximum results. When you have strong performance is the very time to ask, "Can we set an even higher standard?" Concentration is vital, but it's also very risky. You must choose the right concentrations, or—to use a military term—you leave your flanks totally uncovered.

Innovation

You must also look for tomorrow's success, the true innovations, the diversity that stirs the imagination. What are the opportunities, the new conditions, the emerging issues? Do they fit you? Do you really believe in this? But you have to be careful. Before you go into something new, don't say, "This is how we do it." Say, "Let's find out what this requires. What does the customer value? What is the state of the art? How can we make a difference?" Finding answers to these questions is essential.

Risk Taking

Planning always involves decisions on where to take the risks. Some risks you can afford to take—if something goes wrong, it is easily reversible with minor damage.

And some decisions may carry great risk, but you cannot afford *not* to take it. You have to balance the short range with the long. If you are too conservative, you miss the opportunity. If you commit too much too fast, there may not be a long run to worry about. There is no formula for these risk-taking decisions. They are entrepreneurial and uncertain, but they must be made.

Analysis

Finally, in planning it is important to recognize when you do *not* know, when you are not yet sure whether to abandon, concentrate, go into something new, or take a particular risk. Then your objective is to conduct an analysis. Before making the final decision, you study a weak but essential performance area, a challenge on the horizon, the opportunity just beginning to take shape.

Build Understanding and Ownership

The plan begins with a mission. It ends with *action steps* and a *budget*. Action steps establish accountability for objectives—who will do what by when—and the budget commits the resources necessary to implement the plan. To build understanding and ownership for the plan, action steps are developed by the people who will carry them out. Everyone with a role should have the opportunity to give input. This looks incredibly slow. But when the plan is completed, the next day everyone understands it. More people in the organization want the new, are committed to it, are ready to act.

The Self-Assessment Team will prepare the final plan for review by the board. Following presentation and discussion, the board chairman will request approval of the mission, goals, and supporting budget. The chairman may request adoption of a vision statement, if one has been developed, as part of the plan. As soon as approval is given, implementation begins.

Never Really Be Satisfied

This is the last of the self-assessment questions, and your involvement as a participant soon draws to a close. Appraisal will be ongoing. The organization must monitor progress in achieving goals and meeting objectives, and, above all, must measure results in changed lives. You must adjust the plan when conditions change, results are poor, there is a surprise success, or the customer leads you to a place different from where you imagined.

True self-assessment is never finished. Leadership requires constant resharpening, refocusing, never really being satisfied. I encourage you especially to keep asking the question, *What do we want to be remembered for?* It is a question that induces you to renew yourself—and the organization—because it pushes you to see what you can become.

Peter F. Drucker

Figure 1 uses a circular movement to show that evaluation and planning are continuous.

FIGURE 1. PLANNING FOR RESULTS DIAGRAM.

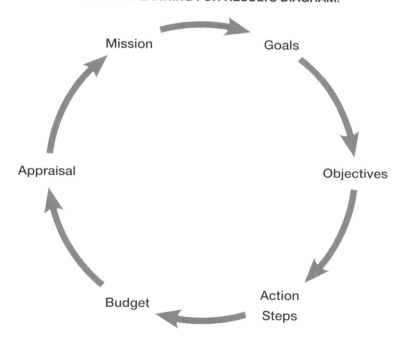

Mission is essential to social sector planning. The mission answers the questions, What is our reason for being? Why do we do what we do? For what, in the end, do we want to be remembered? From the mission flow goals that set the organization's fundamental long-range direction and, together, outline its desired future. Objectives are specific and measurable levels of achievement. Action steps are the detailed plans and activities to meet the objectives; the budget commits necessary resources; and appraisal demonstrates whether objectives are met and results achieved.

Worksheet 5.1:
What Is Our Mission?
(Workshop)

a. The vision is a picture of the organization's desired future. If the organization would like to develop a vision, what is it?

b. The mission answers the questions, What is our reason for being? Does the mission need to be revisited? (Refer to Worksheet 1.2.)

☐ Yes   ☐ No

c. What is our mission?

Worksheet 5.1:
What Is Our Mission?
(Organizational)

a. The vision is a picture of the organization's desired future. If the organization would like to develop a vision, what is it?

b. The mission answers the questions, What is our reason for being? Does the mission need to be revisited? (Refer to Worksheet 1.2.)

☐ Yes   ☐ No

c. What is our mission?

Worksheet 5.2:
What Are Our Goals?
(Workshop)

Goals are a set of three to five aims that set the organization's fundamental, long-range direction.

What are our goals?

1.

2.

3.

4.

5.

Worksheet 5.2:
What Are Our Goals?
(Organizational)

Goals are a set of three to five aims that set the organization's fundamental, long-range direction.

What are our goals?

1.

2.

3.

4.

5.

Worksheet 5.3:
What Is Our Plan to Achieve Results for the Organization? (Workshop)

The mission and goals are approved by the board of directors before the plan is developed. This worksheet serves as a template to help the organization prepare the plan. To better understand the elements of the plan, refer to Figure 1 on page 83.

Goals	Objectives (Measurable)	Action Steps (Measurable)	Budget Implications (Measurable)	Target Date (Completion)	Staffing (Support Needed)
1.					
2.					
3.					

Worksheet 5.3:
What Is Our Plan to Achieve
Results for the Organization? (cont'd)
(Workshop)

Goals	Objectives (Measurable)	Action Steps (Measurable)	Budget Implications (Measurable)	Target Date (Completion)	Staffing (Support Needed)
4.					
5.					

Worksheet 5.3:
What Is Our Plan to Achieve
Results for the Organization?
(Organizational)

The mission and goals are approved by the board of directors before the plan is developed. This worksheet serves as a template to help the organization prepare the plan. To better understand the elements of the plan, refer to Figure 1 on page 83.

Goals	Objectives (Measurable)	Action Steps (Measurable)	Budget Implications (Measurable)	Target Date (Completion)	Staffing (Support Needed)
1.					
2.					
3.					

Goals	Objectives (Measurable)	Action Steps (Measurable)	Budget Implications (Measurable)	Target Date (Completion)	Staffing (Support Needed)
4.					
5.					

How will we communicate our mission, plan, and results to our primary and supporting customers?

How will we communicate our mission, plan, and results to our primary and supporting customers?

Afterword

Effective Implementation of the Plan[9]

Work doesn't get done by a magnificent statement of policy. Work is only done when it's done. Done by people. By people who are properly informed, assigned, and equipped. People with a deadline. People who are developed and evaluated. The best plan is *only* a plan—a set of good intentions—unless there is communication, action, appraisal, and the continuous reallocation of the organization's resources to getting results. The immediate test of a plan is whether leadership actually commits resources to its implementation. Unless such commitment is made, there are only promises and hopes—but no plan.

Communication, Development of People, and Performance

The nonprofit organization must be information-based. Information must flow from the individuals doing the work to the board and management, and it must flow back as well. In a national voluntary organization, the day after the board approved the organization's plan, the chairman was off on a round of visits to local chapters. At each stop she met with leaders and gave speeches focused on vision, mission, goals, and how the local chapter could contribute to results. She answered question after question from individual members and encouraged them to communicate their experience and observations directly to national leadership as time went on. Simultaneously, the executive director held meetings with staff; confirmed new assignments; and led discussion on objectives, action steps, and how progress and achievement would be appraised. The board chairman and chief executive immediately demonstrated their commitment to the plan and set the stage for ongoing communication.

Management emphasis should always be on performance. But, especially for a nonprofit organization, it must also be on developing people. Staff and volunteers require clear assignments that tap their strengths and allow them—through training, encouragement, and the right challenges—to expand these strengths. They need frequent and open opportunities to review team and individual performance. They need leaders and managers who sit down and say, "This is what you and I committed ourselves to. How have we done? What should we do to further your growth?" The guideline is, if people try, work with them. Look for a different way they can contribute. But if a person cannot perform, another assignment should be considered. The alternative is that all those who have to work with the person lose their capacity to contribute. Without management resolve in these difficult situations, the plan becomes hollow.

Appraisal Is All Important

What we measure and how we measure it determines what will be considered relevant and thereby determines not just what we see but what we—and others—do. Monitoring should be built in early, involve people at all levels of the organization, and give leadership the ability to quickly take corrective action or move to build on success. There must be systematic feedback—a way of self-control from events back to planning.

Your plan commits present resources to the uncertainties of the future. This, according to elementary probability mathematics, means some decisions will prove to be wrong. Adjusting them requires two things: first, that you think through alternatives ahead of time so that you have something to fall back on, and second, that you build into the plan the responsibility for bailing it out instead of arguing about who made what mistakes.

When a new tactic or action doesn't seem to be working, the rule is, "If at first you don't succeed, try once more." Stop and ask what has been learned. Try to improve the strategy, to change it, and to make another major effort. Maybe, although I am reluctant to encourage it, you should make a third effort. After that, go to work where the results are.

Appraisal should not focus on flaws and mistakes at the expense of achievement. There is a tendency to devote the most time to problem solving, to pour more and more into rescuing a failure. When you have results, communicate them, give recognition where it is due, and reward effectiveness. Take time to analyze what has gone *right,* how even better results might be achieved, how success in one area can be translated to others.

At the same time, bear in mind that no success is forever. It is far more difficult to abandon yesterday's success than it is to reappraise failure. Success breeds its own hubris. It creates emotional attachment, habits of mind and action, and, above all, false self-confidence. A success that has outlived its usefulness—and today this happens very quickly—may, in the end, be more damaging than failure.

Mission Is the Star to Steer By

A plan is a framework, not a formula. When conditions change, when complex decisions must be made, first ask, "What will further the mission?" Then look to goals, to what results should and *could* be. The greatest mistake when implementing a plan is to allow objectives to become a straitjacket; commitment to mission and goals is long term, but one always makes compromises on tactics.

I know of a public health organization that was approached by a school system asking for a partnership, a means for that public health organization to take a prevention program directly into the classroom and reach children—the primary customers—quickly and in great numbers. They struggled over the opportunity because "it wasn't in the plan," and their people were already working on a different approach. It took open minds and managerial agility to change direction, to take the entrepreneurial risk and abandon an objective mid-course in favor of a more effective one.

My hope, as you complete this formal process, is that you do not stop with "what is in the plan" but make true self-assessment an ongoing practice. This means constant scanning of the environment, continual learning from the customer. It means appraisal, countless small adjustments, and the courage to make major change. True self-assessment creates, through dedication and hard work, that flow of knowledge throughout the organization that strengthens judgment, renews leadership, and inspires vision. It is the foundation of excellence in performance.

Peter F. Drucker

Glossary of Terms

ACTION STEPS Detailed plans and activities that meet an organization's objectives.

APPRAISAL Process for monitoring progress in meeting objectives and achieving results; point at which the action steps for meeting objectives may be modified on the basis of experience or changed conditions.

BUDGET The commitment of resources necessary to implement plans—the financial expression of a particular plan of work.

CONCENTRATION Strengthening what works. The organization focuses on the programs and activities that contribute to achieving the right results.

CONSTRUCTIVE DISSENT Using dissent or disagreement as an opportunity to "[create] understanding and mutual respect."[10]

CUSTOMER VALUE That which satisfies customers' needs (physical and psychological well-being), wants (where, when, and how service or product is provided), and aspirations (desired future results).

CUSTOMERS Those who must be satisfied in order for the organization to achieve results. The *primary customer* is the person whose life is changed through the organization's work. *Supporting customers* are volunteers, members, partners, funders, referral sources, staff, and others who must be satisfied in order for the organization to achieve results.

DEPTH INTERVIEWS One-on-one interviews used to highlight the insights of a select group of individuals inside the organization. Interview findings provide a touchstone for facilitated discussion and decision making.

ENVIRONMENTAL SCAN To find and identify change . . . by examining the sources and direction of change as they become evident through [research] media, publications, and individual observation and experience.[11]

GOALS A set of three to five aims that set the organization's fundamental, future direction.

INNOVATION Change that creates a new dimension of performance.[12]

INTERNAL DATA Summarized information regarding the history, present status, and performance of the organization.

LEADERSHIP TEAM The chairman of the board and the chief executive officer of the organization. Both lead organizational self-assessment.

MISSION The organization's reason for being, its purpose. Says what, in the end, the organization wants to be remembered for.

OBJECTIVES Specific and measurable levels of achievement that move an organization toward its goals.

PLAN A concise summation of the organization's purpose and future direction. The plan encompasses vision, mission, goals, objectives, action steps, a budget, and appraisal.[13]

PLANNED ABANDONMENT Removing or stopping programs and activities that are decreasing in relevance or not producing adequate results.

QUALITATIVE MEASURES Address the depth and breadth of change within a particular context. The measures begin with specific observations; build toward patterns; and tell a subtle, individualized story.[14]

QUANTITATIVE MEASURES Use definitive standards. The measures begin with categories and expectations and tell an objective story.[15]

RESULTS The organization's bottom line. Defined in changed lives—behavior, circumstances, health, hopes, competence, or capacity. Results are always outside the organization.

TREND A statement of the direction of change.[16]

VISION A picture of the organization's desired future when the organization's goals are achieved and its mission accomplished.

Notes

1. *The Drucker Foundation Self-Assessment Tool: Participant Workbook,* Revised Edition (San Francisco: Jossey-Bass, 1999), pp. 3–6.

2. 1999 *Participant Workbook,* pp. 14–16.

3. *The Five Most Important Questions You Will Ever Ask About Your Nonprofit Organization: Participant's Workbook* (San Francisco: Jossey-Bass, 1993), p. 13.

4. 1999 *Participant Workbook,* p. 16.

5. 1999 *Participant Workbook,* pp. 22–24.

6. 1999 *Participant Workbook,* pp. 32–34.

7. 1999 *Participant Workbook,* pp. 40–44.

8. 1999 *Participant Workbook,* pp. 52–56.

9. 1999 *Participant Workbook,* pp. 59–61.

10. Peter F. Drucker, *Managing the Nonprofit Organization: Principles and Practices* (New York: HarperCollins, 1990), p. 125.

11. James G. Dalton, Jennifer Jarratt, and John B. Mahaffie, *From Scan to Plan: Integrating Trends into the Strategy-Making Process: Executive Summary* (Washington, D.C.: Foundation of the American Society of Association Executives, 2003), p. 12.

12. Peter F. Drucker, *Innovation and Entrepreneurship, Practice and Principles* (New York: Harper & Row, 1985).

13. 1999 *Participant Workbook,* p. 52.

14. 1999 *Participant Workbook,* p. 41.

15. 1999 *Participant Workbook,* p. 41.

16. Dalton, Jarratt, and Mahaffie, *From Scan to Plan,* p. 4.

About Frances Hesselbein

Frances Hesselbein is the president and CEO of the Leader to Leader Institute (formerly the Peter F. Drucker Foundation for Nonprofit Management) and its founding president. In 1998, Mrs. Hesselbein was awarded the Presidential Medal of Freedom, the highest civilian honor in the United States of America. The award recognized her leadership as CEO of Girl Scouts of the U.S.A. from 1976–1990, her role as the founding president of the Drucker Foundation, and her service as a pioneer for women, volunteerism, diversity, and opportunity. President George H. W. Bush appointed her to two Presidential commissions on national and community service.

In 2009, Mrs. Hesselbein was appointed the *Class of 1951 Chair for the Study of Leadership* at the United States Military Academy at West Point's Department of Behavioral Sciences and Leadership. She is the first woman and first non-graduate to serve in this chair. Also in 2009, the University of Pittsburgh initiated *The Hesselbein Global Academy for Student Leadership and Civic Engagement.* The Academy aims to develop a cadre of experienced, ethical leaders equipped to address critical issues throughout the world.

Mrs. Hesselbein serves on many nonprofit and corporate boards, including Mutual of America Life Insurance Company; Bright China Social Fund; American Express Philanthropy; the Center for Social Initiative, Harvard Business School; the Hauser Center for Nonprofit Management, Harvard Kennedy School; the Graduate School of International Relations and Pacific Studies, University of California, San Diego; and the Alliance Advisory Council for the Center for Creative Leadership. She was the Chairman of Volunteers of America from 2002–2006.

Mrs. Hesselbein was duly honored with a Lifetime Award for her exceptional work as former CEO of Girl Scouts of the U.S.A. and her continued commitment to developing leaders of all ages. She was inducted into the Enterprising Women Hall of Fame at the 7th Annual Enterprising Women of the Year Awards Celebration. She is the recipient of twenty honorary doctoral degrees.

In 2008, Mrs. Hesselbein was presented with the International Leadership Association's Lifetime Achievement Award and the Tempo International Leadership Award. In this same year, she was named a Senior Leader at the United States Military

Academy National Conference on Ethics in America. In 2007, Mrs. Hesselbein was awarded the John F. Kennedy Memorial Fellowship by Fulbright New Zealand. In 2003, she was the first recipient of the Dwight D. Eisenhower National Security Award.

Mrs. Hesselbein is editor-in-chief of the award-winning quarterly journal *Leader to Leader*, and a coeditor of a book of the same name. She is the author of *Hesselbein on Leadership* and with General Eric K. Shinseki, introduced *Be*Know*Do: Leadership the Army Way*. Mrs. Hesselbein is the coeditor of 27 books in 29 languages.

Acknowledgments

We are deeply grateful to the leaders, facilitators, and organizations that have contributed their time, inquisitiveness, and expertise to the third edition of *The Five Most Important Questions Self-Assessment Tool*. Over one hundred leaders representing more than seventy organizations helped field test the *Tool*.

We thank the leaders and facilitators who have worked tirelessly to bring Peter Drucker's *Self-Assessment Tool* to the social sector. We would like to thank Constance Rossum for her assistance in developing the first edition and Gary Stern for assisting in developing the second edition. Among the many individuals who helped shape the third edition are Derek Bell, Theresa Berenato, Dee Ann Boyd, Risa Cohn, Cathy Crosky, Susan Diamond, Carla Grantham, Justine Green, Lawrence Greenspan, Kathy Long Holland, Lee Igel, Irv Katz, Patricia Lewis, Matthew MacPherson, Michael Millar, Maria Carpenter Ort, Peggy Morrison Outon, Katherina Rosqueta, Doug Schallau, Kevin S. Smith, Iain Somerville, Bonita and Mark Thompson, Robert Clifford Uerz, and Tamara Woodbury.

Special thanks go to Frances Hesselbein for her guidance and her commitment to the social sector and performance excellence; she has been a tireless champion for Peter Drucker's work and for bringing The Five Most Important Questions to the social sector. Our appreciation goes to Jesse Wiley, our editorial partner at Jossey-Bass/Wiley, as well as to Susan Rachmeler and Nina Kreiden, who helped develop and produce the publications there. We thank Cathey Brown and Claire Walden for their work developing, editing, and field testing this revised edition.

We would like to thank the Bright China Social Fund and the Buford Foundation for their generosity in making this edition of the *Tool* possible. We also thank the American Management Association and the Women Presidents' Organization for supporting The Five Most Important Questions workshops.

Our final thanks go to Peter F. Drucker for his dedication to the effective organization, for his contributions to management literature and practices, and for his support and contributions to the social sector. Without him, his wisdom and his passion, Leader to Leader would not exist and publishing these materials would not be possible.

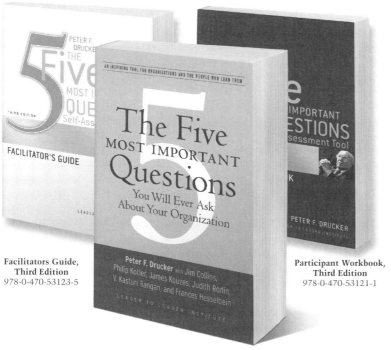